Date due

91 06 24			
91 06 19			

TO THE MUNICIPAL ELECTORS OF INVERNESS.

GENTLEMEN,

Solon, the celebrated legislator of Athens, history informs us, enacted a law for the capital punishment of every citizen who should continue neuter when parties ran high in that republic. He considered, it should seem, the declining to take a decided part on great and critical emergencies as a proof of such culpable indifference to the interests of the commonwealth as could be expiated only by death. While we blame the rigour of this law, we must confess the principle on which it was founded is just and solid. It may be that in some political contests, relating to particular men or factions, a well wisher to his country may be permitted to remain silent, but when the vital interests of a union or community are at stake, it becomes every man to act with firmness and vigour. I consider the present as an occasion of this nature, and shall, therefore, make no apology for laying before you some considerations it has suggested. The union between a representative and his constituents ought to be strict and entire, and it is an important question for the electors, whether candidates for their suffrage be of that character to warrant the belief that this union shall be formed on such a basis as to be permanent. A word or two in detail will be necessary to set this view in a clearer light, and let me first address myself, as first in order and destitution as regards representatives, to the electors of the

FIRST WARD.

This important portion of the constituency may be said for some time back to have but a mockery of a representation. Last year, two gentlemen of whom great hopes were entertained, Mr Thomson and Dr Nicol, were elected, but the former has cut the Council, and the latter's personal and professional avocations are too multifarious to allow him time for extra municipal duties. The other representatives, or rather misrepresentatives of this Ward are, Donald Fraser, junior, Thomas Mackintosh, Kenneth Ross, and Andrew Fraser. The mere fact of being governed by such men, every elector must feel absolutely degrading to him as a man—still more degrading to him as an Invernessian—as a citizen of that town, which, as the capital of the Highlands should be an example to the northern burghs. The first and third of these Nincompoops were permitted for a time to bring into contempt in their persons the office of magistrates, but his colleagues got so thoroughly ashamed of the former that they refused to walk to church with him, and the very first opportunity was taken to kick the other out of the seat of honour. The second and fourth also attempted to outrage decency by forcing themselves into office—the former aspiring to a bailieship, and the latter Andrew Fraser, with unparalleled audacity, stretching out his greasy and rosin-covered hand to grasp the Treasurership and the burgh purse. Thanks to the majority of the Council, the community were saved from this crowning degradation.

The three years' race of two of this imbecile crew has just terminated, and it was believed that they would not be foolhardy enough to court further uncariable notoriety by thrusting themselves forward as candidates for an office, their qualifications and talents for which would disgrace the lowest hero of a village school. But it seems their presumption is equal to their incapacity, and Kenneth Ross and Andrew Fraser have the effrontery to solicit permission for other three years to play their "fantastic tricks" and again to put in jeopardy the prosperity and respectability of the town.

Each of these political charlatans is but a spawn spewed out by popular excitement, yet on this very circumstance they found their claim to your suffrages. Kenneth Ross, in his card, says that he was the first to take steps to prevent the sale of the Town Lands; and in support of this bold assertion reprints resolutions he moved at a meeting held on the subject in Oct, 1842. This statement is utterly unfounded. I was present at that meeting; and I remember the circumstances perfectly well. By his card Kenneth makes himself appear as moving the resolutions. But he did not write them, nor could he do so; and, in fact, when moving them, another person was obliged to READ them for him. Neither the meeting nor resolutions originated with him; and neither he nor Andrew Fraser, whose rabid tongue is blistered with unctuous rage against educational institutions, could write a motion any more than they could Shakspeure's Hamlet or Milton's Paradise Lost. Justice, however, compels me to state that Andrew, once at the Council table, made the attempt with a red-heel kilavine, but failed, and has never since ventured another essay.

But I'll tell you what originated with K. R. He proposed to make markets in the river Ness, behind the Caledonian Hotel stables—the only original idea that ever entered his benighted brains—and with this crotchet he has, meeting after meeting, for three years, literally bored the Council. Poor Kenny! whenever I see your name, associated as it is with this ridiculous project, I invariably think of Bigdum-Funidos, Hokey-Pokey

or Mundungus, Blue Beard, Nym, Pym, and Bardolph, and a whole host of absurd associations. If you must be in water, let a large watering-pot be constructed, on four wheels, and painted a jolly green, with the word "Pure" in water colours. Put Andrew up the spout, with his handsome face just appearing above the orifice; let yourself sit like Midas on the little ledge possessed by every well conducted watering pot with a little ladle to lade out the "Pure" to whoever may ask for it. The machine may be drawn by Andrew's canvassers, with their heads in sacks, so that they may not be seen. This will pay you better than all your speculations in bubble railways.

Kenneth Ross refers to the past as a guarantee for his future conduct, but unfortunately the river has not left him a shred to cover the nakedness of his character; the Chamberlain's book, however, will show that he wasted a large sum of the town's money on workmen he employed in the river opposite the pier without the authority or even knowledge of the Council. This "pure" job cost about L.150, and has not been productive of one farthing's worth of benefit to the town.

Of his propensity to throw public money upon the waters it has been considered hopeless to cure him; but, fortunately from among Dr Nicol's paper's, supposed to have been entirely lost in the late calamitous fire, a scrap has been found in the ruins which relates to, and contains his advice in, a case of obstinate hydrocephalus, and for the benefit of Hokey-Pokey and Merry Andrew, I have translated the passage from the original Latin. The Doctor says— "Pay great attention to the patient's pulse, and embrocate it with a mild solution of carbonate of antimony—even oxymuriate of potassium carefully granulated may be found an advisable detergent. The patient being duly secured, and diachylon poultice being applied, make an incision between the cyclomital procep and the ampulla, continuing it in a slanting direction as far as the pleura. Then exhibit caustic until the parietal bone becomes clavicular, and dissect the ovaries. Take up the ligaments and tie the neuralgia, leaving the tendon Achilles in its natural position. Should tetanus ensue, foment with milk and water, and on the third day puncture the pericardium near the hinterian capsule. On the fifth day exhibit mercury and subluxate of quinine, a ter which the treatment must be determined by the general character of the patient's system. Should all these means fail, let him be placed in cold water up to the chin—a river—the Ness, for instance, where it has a curve, as opposite the Caledonian Stables, would be most likely to prove efficacious."

But should Kenneth Ross be cured of this disease, he is so deeply infected with this speculating murrain and law mania, that even if he had the abilities, he has not the time to attend to public matters; and out of sheer compassion to one in his deplorable situation, the electors should leave him to put his own house and affairs in order before allowing him to take charge of theirs.

Andrew Fraser is, if possible, still more destitute of anything to recommend him. His very first vote in the Council was a barefaced and open violation of a solemn pledge. The meeting that was held in the Old Court-room, calling upon him, in consequence, to resign, and his ignominious recantation on the occasion must be fresh in the recollection of the electors, and ought for ever to expunge his name from the list of candidates to represent them in Council. From the vote for reducing the fees in Bell's School he sneaked away, as he did last year at the election of magistrates.

It is true, he may bluster stereotype blarney about the corn-laws and corn plasters, for which he is or was an agent, and so forth, like Councillor Strut, of whom it is recorded, that

"All that he said, and all that he sung,
Was said and sung in the Yorkshire tongue."

But his disgusting vulgarity—his presumptuous arrogance—his personal appearance, garnished with ebony rings encircling his finger nails, and a gold chain displayed over his vest—his consummate ignorance— and his audacious rashness as a corn doctor, place him on a rank with the Therapeutan quacks and gypsies of Egypt, and prove him unfit for the situation of assistant police officer. Enough, however, has been said of him. Let him not again be such a blockhead as to sin against an express proverb—"ne sutor ultra crepidam." And now

— Spare him, ye critics, his foilles are past,
For the Cobbler is come, as he ought, to his last."

I had fully intended to offer a few remarks on the merits of some of the candidates in the second and third Wards; and I may, perhaps, still find it necessary to do so, but, meantime, I will leave the "fires" there raging, to extinguish themselves.

I am, Gentlemen,

Yours to command,

ANDREW FERARA.

REMINISCENCES OF INVERNESS.

EDINBURGH : PRINTED BY JAMES SKINNER AND COMPANY.

INVERNESS FROM THE NORTH END OF CULDUTHIEL ROAD.

REMINISCENCES OF
INVERNESS:

ITS PEOPLE AND PLACES.

BY

JOHN FRASER.

PUBLISHED BY THE AUTHOR,
AT 15 UNION STREET, INVERNESS.
1905.

CONTENTS.

CHAPTER I.

PAGE

CASTLE STREET — THE RECRUITING STATION — EXCHANGE— BRIDGE STREET—WINE SHOP—CASTLE TOLMIE—HIGH STREET, ... 1

CHAPTER II.

PETTY STREET—STEPHEN'S BRAE—INGLIS STREET—LOCHGORM, 7

CHAPTER III.

NEW STREET—ROYAL ACADEMY—CHAPEL OF EASE—DR. BELL'S INSTITUTION—ROSE STREET—ROSE STREET FOUNDRY, . 12

CHAPTER IV.

THE LONGMAN ROAD—NEW STREET—THE GASWORKS—CHAPEL STREET—CHAPELYARD BURYING-GROUND, . . 18

CHAPTER V.

CHAPEL STREET (continued)—GREYFRIARS' BURYING-GROUND— FRIARS' STREET—FACTORY STREET—MAGGOT—WATER- LOO PLACE—JOHN ORDE'S CIRCUS, . . . 24

CHAPTER VI.

SHORE STREET—PORTLAND PLACE—OLD QUAY—THE LAUNCH —NEW QUAY—LOTLAND PLACE, . . . 30

CHAPTER VII.

CROMWELL'S FORT—THE ROPE AND SAIL WORKS—COLONEL FITCH'S HOUSE, ... 36

CHAPTER VIII.

THE BLACK BRIDGE—ANDERSON STREET—GRANT STREET— PUMPGATE STREET—LOWER KESSOCK STREET, . 44

CHAPTER IX.

CAPEL INCH—THORNBUSH—THE WINDMILL, . . . 51

CHAPTER X.

WINDMILL (*continued*)—KESSOCK FERRY, . . . 56

CHAPTER XI.

CLACHNAHARRY — CALEDONIAN CANAL — MONUMENT — THE WELL—MUIRTOWN HOUSE—MUIRTOWN BRIDGE, . 62

CHAPTER XII.

MUIRTOWN HOUSE (*continued*)—CANAL BASIN—MUIRTOWN HOTEL AND WHARF, ... 70

CHAPTER XIII.

THE MUIRTOWN ROPEWORK—TELFORD—MUIRTOWN NURSERIES —TELFORD ROAD—ABBAN STREET, . . . 77

CHAPTER XIV.

HUNTLY STREET—HUNTLY PLACE—VETERAN ROW—TANNERY, 83

CHAPTER XV.

WELLS' FOUNDRY—WELLS STREET—FRIARS' SHOTT, . . 88

CHAPTER XVI.

FRIARS' SHOTT (*continued*), ... 94

CHAPTER XVII.

GREEN OF MUIRTOWN—DAVIS SQUARE—JOHN MACLEAN'S STORY, 99

CHAPTER XVIII.

CELT STREET—HUNTLY STREET—DISPENSARY, . . 105

CHAPTER XIX.

QUEEN STREET—CENTRAL SCHOOL—PRINCES PLACE—BLUE
HOUSE—WEST CHURCH, ... 111

CHAPTER XX.

HUNTLY STREET (*continued*), ... 119

CHAPTER XXI.

KING STREET, ... 125

CHAPTER XXII.

TOMNAHURICH STREET, ... 130

CHAPTER XXIII.

YOUNG STREET—BRIDGE END—NESS WALK—LITTLE GREEN, 136

CHAPTER XXIV.

NESS WALK (*continued*)—BALLIFEARY LANE—TOMNAHURICH
BRIDGE, ... 142

CHAPTER XXV.

THE LITTLE GREEN, ... 150

CHAPTER XXVI.

TANNER'S LANE, ... 157

CHAPTER XXVII.

STONE BRIDGE—"TOM TIT'S" STORY, ... 164

CHAPTER XXVIII.

Stone Bridge (*continued*)—Queen Mary's Visit—"Tom Tit's" Story (*continued*)—Bridge Street, . . . 172

CHAPTER XXIX.

Top of Bridge Street—The Steeple—"Tom Tit's" Story (*concluded*), ... 180

CHAPTER XXX.

Church Street, ... 188

CHAPTER XXXI.

Church Street (*continued*)—High Church and Church-yard—Gaelic Church, ... 202

CHAPTER XXXII.

Bank Street—"Courier" Office—Ness Bank—The Haugh —View Place, ... 212

CHAPTER XXXIII.

North End of Culduthel Road—Castle Hill—Castle Wynd—Exchange, ... 223

CHAPTER XXXIV.

The Great Flood, January 25th, 1849, . . . 236

ILLUSTRATIONS.

Inverness from the North End of Culduthel Road, *Frontispiece*

The Black Bridge, ... 45

The Castle and Stone Bridge from Douglas Row, . 163

A WALK THROUGH INVERNESS
SIXTY YEARS AGO.

CHAPTER I.

CASTLE STREET—THE RECRUITING STATION—EXCHANGE—
BRIDGE STREET—WINE SHOP—CASTLE TOLMIE—HIGH
STREET.

As Invernessians, old and young, are ever anxious to
hear of bygone days in the Capital, it is with much
pleasure I give the following reminiscences in the form
of a walk through Inverness over half a century ago.
As will be observed, the stroll begins at the head of
Castle Street, known of old as Doomsdale Street, and
with genial good humour our guide conducts us through
the "auld toon," pointing out persons and objects of
interest by the way. He begins thus:—

On the right hand corner at the top of Castle Street
is the shop occupied by Mr. Noble, cartwright (grandfather of Mr. Noble, The White House). About half-
way down the street to the right is the shop of Mr. William Ross, painter (father of our present genial Provost).
Mr. Ross has always a smile and a kind word to all his
acquaintances. There, he has just entered into conver-

A

sation with Mr. John Bond, the new editor of the *Inverness Herald*,—the office just being within the entry. Mr. Bond has recently come to town from Hastings, and already takes a warm interest in the history and folk-lore of the town.   On the opposite side of the street is the shop of Bailie Alexander Shaw, baker (now Mr. Myrtle's).   Mr. Shaw is a keen politician, and is always on the look-out for the latest tit-bit in the way of Parliamentary news.   Further down on the right are the shops of Mr. Nicholas Hardie, stoneware merchant, and Mr. Alexander Smith, hairdresser.   The latter gentleman was the first to introduce photography into Inverness.   There is a good old citizen, Mr. Alexander Forbes, chemist, standing at the door of his shop, Mr. George Galloway, his assistant, being meanwhile busily engaged behind the counter.   That clerical-looking gentleman you see sitting just inside the door is Parson Duncan Mackenzie of the Episcopal Church, Strathnairn, who is able to minister not only to the souls but to the bodies of frail humanity.   His advice is very much sought after by the sick poor, who are always very grateful.   Yonder on the opposite side of the street is Phineas Mackintosh emerging from his residence.   He is a ready conversationalist, and is ever willing to crack a joke with the latest comer.   See yonder group at the bottom of the street; they are gathered round the Recruiting Station, next close to the Peahen and at the back of the old Town Hall.   It is market day, and the recruiting party are getting under way to beat up.   Sergeant Simon Fraser, who had the unique distinction of enlisting nearly a whole regiment, is already there, along with his satellite, Red Rory the piper, from whose rubicund countenance one would infer that he is particularly partial to his native mountain dew. (Poor Rory!   When " war's shrill blast was blawn" he was sent to the Crimea, where he soon fell a victim to the climate.) We are now in full view of the Exchange, and groups of country women, quaintly attired with shawls, white mutches, and cloaks, are here exposing their produce, consisting of butter, eggs, fowls, and fir candles. That loquacious female, attired in a short skirt and a very old-world cap, with lugs on it that might adorn any elephant, is known as "Suebac." She is the spouse of the custodian of the reading-room below the Town Hall. The Town Hall, by the way, was formerly the residence of Lord Lovat, and has been used for municipal purposes since 1716. Captain Burt, in his letters from Inverness, 1743, describes it as being a noisy rendezvous of the townsmen.

The usual habitues of the Exchange are beginning to assemble. John Fraser (Saighdear Dhu) is already there doing his morning exercise. His left leg, you will observe, is rather stiff in consequence of his wound at Quatre Bras. The old man still delights to fraternise with his military friends. We are now passing down Bridge Street, and in front of the Police Office we pause for a moment while we stand over the grave of the last criminal hung in Inverness—John Adams, who was executed in 1835.

(Parenthetically we may remark that the bones have since been reinterred, and are now lying below the steps of the present Police Office in the Castle Wynd.)

That stout official you see with prisoner in hand is John Macbean, the thief-catcher, who has arrived from an expedition. The town officers—Sandy Grant (Supple Sandy), James Tallach, and William Chisholm—are looking on, and preparing for their day's work. There on the right is the office and wine vaults of ex-Provost Ferguson. Yes! there is the genial Provost himself coming down the outside steps of the office in conversation with Captain Fraser of Culduthel. This is the oldest business in town, it being established in 1727. Towards the old stone bridge may be observed, on the steps of Castle Tolmie, the burly vintner, John Fraser, popularly known as "Jock Beef." Through a narrow way leading to the back of Castle Tolmie we observe the ruins of the house that was said to be occupied by Queen Mary in 1562.

We will now retrace our steps up Bridge Street. That distinguished-looking gentleman is John Mackenzie, banker, Ness House, father of Mrs. Grogan, well known in literary circles. Over the way we see the portly figure of Mr. James Simpson, accompanied by his beautiful mastiff. We are now again on High Street, and are just at the shop of Mr. Kenneth MacRae (site of present Caledonian Bank), known as "Kenny A'things." His only customer at present, as will be observed, is Dunk Colloden, the heckler, and a heckler he is and no mistake. He has just asked Dunk, "What do you want, Dunk, for we have everything here?" "Well," is Dunk's reply, "I want a penny loaf." Almost opposite is Mr. James Smith, bookseller, in earnest conversation with Charles Robertson ("Dandie Charlie"), the Beau Brummell of Inverness, whose trim appearance makes him the cynosure of all eyes. See, there is Mr. Donald Macdougall of the Tartan Warehouse, attired in his cross-cut tartan trousers and tall white hat, entering his shop. He appears in very good humour this morning, doubtless on account of his having obtained a large order from Balmoral. That shop with the cured pig and the orange in its mouth is that of Mr. Angus Macbean, grocer, who is remarkable for the trim manner in which he keeps his establishment. No. 8, opposite, is Mr.

Hugh Snowie, who is conversing in front of his establishment with the Duke of Richmond. Look! there is the mail coach. It has just arrived from the south, and is landing its passengers at the Union Hotel. We are now at the Post Office, the whole staff of which consists of four individuals. There is an old veteran coming down the Market Brae, John Macfarlane. Poor old chap! He lost his leg at Waterloo. We are now in Petty Street, which recently resumed its old name of East Gate. See that old blind soldier coming along there, he is leaning on the arm of his grandson,—he is Davie Gordon, who lost his sight on the banks of the Nile with Sir Ralph Abercrombie in 1800. We have now reached the east end of the street, and we are in the centre of the Fish Market.

NOTE.—It may not be generally known that until the middle of the eighteenth century Castle Street was known as "Domesdale Street," it being the way by which convicts were led from the Tolbooth on Bridge Street to the place of execution in the vicinity of Muirfield, the exact spot being a small knoll, located a few years ago in course of excavations for building purposes. Until about forty-five years ago there was in the middle of Castle Street a very unsightly and dangerous brae, the side path being high above the streetway. Its removal was the first step that led towards the great improvements that have since taken place in that important thoroughfare. When our local bank—the Caledonian—was inaugurated in 1838, its head office was the shop now occupied by Mr. Walton, draper. In 1849 the company removed to their present commodious premises. In a small shop, formerly used by Mr. W. Smith, bookseller, as a stationery store, just on the spot where the entrance to the Y.M.C.A. now is, there lived many years ago two aged sisters. They sold small wares such as needles, pins, and tape, and occasionally pot barley. They were very retired, being seldom seen beyond the threshold of their small shop. Being once asked if they ever ventured to take a walk into the country, "Oh, yes!" was the reply of one of the ladies, "we were once up as far as the big trees at Kingsmills." The ladies lived to a patriarchal age, and bequeathed the sum of £600 to the Guildry Incorporation of Inverness, a fund that is still a help to many needy townspeople.

CHAPTER II.

PETTY STREET—STEPHEN'S BRAE—INGLIS STREET—
LOCHGORM.

WE are now at the Fish Market at the east end of Petty Street. On the right you observe that large enclosure which has been for many years used as the depôt for the carriers of goods from Perth in the south and Aberdeen in the east. They have stated days of arrival and departure, heavier goods coming round by ship to the harbour. While I have been making this observation Tibbie Main has just made her daily purchase of the defunct finny denizens of the deep for disposal through the town without much choice; everything is fish that comes into her barrow, be they cat-fish, dog-fish, or any other kind. While this is going on, Donald Fraser, who has been for many years bellman, is with stentorian voice announcing that there is "fresh fish in the market." "Peggy Cubbart" now comes on the scene. She is anxious to make a bargain for a fresh haddock for dinner for her husband, Jock Spindles, herself, and her brother William, who are well-known knights of St. Crispin. As you look into Peggy's time-worn face you see at once that she is the scion of a noble family. Would you be surprised to know that the old woman is among the last of the Cuthberts of Castlehill, a family that for centuries was held in high esteem in Inverness and the surrounding district; but, alas! it is little heard of now. Listen! "Yellow sand all the way from Petty!" That

is the voice of a well-known character who earns a
precarious livelihood by retailing sand to the Inverness
housewives for scouring purposes.

There are but few buildings beyond this point save
the Lochgorm Inn, which may be termed "the last
shift," so we may retrace our steps.   We are now at
the foot of Stephen's Brae, and that handsome equipage
which you see coming down the brae and passing on
our left is the magnificent silver-mounted coach—
"The Silver Coach"—drawn by two splendid horses
gorgeously harnessed.   Mr. Robertson, the coachman,
sits proudly on the "the dicky."   The coach belongs
to the laird of Abertarff.   Inside is Mrs. Fraser (who is
a sister of Cluny Macpherson), together with her
beautiful daughter.   See ! the coach now draws up at the
door of Mr. Andrew Smith, draper, High Street.   That
amiable-looking gentleman you see coming along on
foot is Abertarff himself, great-grandson of Simon
Lord Lovat, and, as you will observe, he seems in
manner and deportment every inch a Highland chief
and a Fraser.   His town residence is the Crown House,
where his hospitality is proverbial.   We are now at the
Inverness Journal office, and that gentleman you see
through the window is Mr. M'Donald, the editor.
These other two men you observe busily engaged inside
are Mr. Hutcheson, foreman printer, and Mr. Peter
Mackintosh, foreman compositor, both of whom take a
great interest in the temperance movement in town
That was Mr. Alexander Jack, bootmaker, who just
wished us " Good morning."   He has had the honour
of being appointed bootmaker to the Prince Consort.
We have now reached an old hostelry known as the
Rob Roy Inn, which is beginning to be well patronised,
particularly on market days.   Over the way is Theatre
Lane, now Hamilton Street.   In that small building

next to the smithy is held a weekly prayer meeting in connection with the Chapel of Ease. These meetings are largely attended, and have been held there from time immemorial. We are now at the building known as Castle Raat, situated on Theatre Lane. Then we come to Inglis Street, which is so called after a popular chief magistrate of the beginning of the century—Provost Inglis of Kingsmills, whose name is so familiar in connection with the building of the Northern Infirmary. A few doors on the left you observe a small house; it was there that Edward Strathern Gordon (Lord Gordon) first saw the light in 1814. His father (Major Gordon) was a long time abroad, and he, Edward, was educated at the Inverness Royal Academy along with Dr. Kennedy of Stepney, with whom he is on terms of close friendship. Right opposite Gordon's birthplace is the shop of Mr. Charles Crotchie, whose portly appearance is much admired. He is just conducting a sale inside his premises of an article of virtu. Mr. Crotchie is a Frenchman, and it is a well-known fact that he was one of Napoleon's Imperial Guards, and fought at Waterloo. He is concluding his sale in broken English with his usual phrase, "Are you all doon? Are you all doon? Vell, I'm doon too." On the right is the building which, until recently, was occupied as the Theatre Royal of Inverness, Tom Ryder, the well-known actor, occupying the boards for many seasons with considerable success. The last building on the right is the Wesleyan Chapel, which was erected toward the close of the last century, services being held three times each Sunday. The minister is the Rev. Mr. Hooley, an able preacher and an ardent temperance advocate. The services of the little chapel are well attended, particularly in the evenings, the latter being remarkably popular among the young people. On the opposite side of the street to the chapel is a group of small thatched houses with windows in the roof, one of them being occupied as a general store by Mr. Peter Gibson, father of the late Bailie Gibson. We are now on what is known as New Street (Academy Street); but as we feel that the "inner man" is making a demand on us, we will adjourn for luncheon.

NOTE.—At the east end of Petty Street, just beyond the Carriers' Depôt, there were at this time several houses of unknown antiquity. There was a high retaining wall immediately below Abertarff House, between which and the roadway there was a kind of "Tom Tiddlers" ground, where now stands a block of stately buildings. On the other side of the road, the site of Messrs. Macdonald & Fraser's saleyard, there was an unsightly loch of stagnant water, hence the name Lochgorm ("Green Loch"). It was in a park about 200 yards north of Lochgorm Inn that the first turf of the Inverness and Nairn Railway was cut by Caroline, Dowager Countess of Seafield, assisted by the late Mr. E. W. Mackintosh of Raigmore, on the 22nd September 1854. In the old coaching days the Lords of Justiciary used to break their journey at Raigmore House, and dine with the genial laird. Then followed a state entry into the town in the evening. This took place twice a year, in April and September, when the townspeople went to Lochgorm to receive the Court. For a considerable time before the arrival of the Court every coign of vantage was taken possession of, and the vast crowd anxiously waited the formation of the procession, which was preceded by the town's officers in ancient costume, bearing their time-honoured insignia of authority, the halberts. They were followed by the Provost, Bailies, Town-Councillors, Established

Church ministers, and the Sheriffs of the Northern Counties, the latter wearing court dress swords. Then followed the Queen's trumpeters, mounted, then the judges in a close carriage, drawn by four grey horses, with outriders in scarlet jackets and buff breeches. In later times there was a band of music and a guard of honour. On the arrival of the procession at the Caledonian Hotel, and while their lordships were alighting, the trumpeters rang out a " fanfare," which to the boyish imagination seemed to say—

> " All who are innocent they need not fear,
> All who are guilty they may prepare."

We may here venture to add that we believe the abolition of this custom was the snapping of one of the last links that bound us to the feudal times.

In October 1846 there occurred at Castle Raat one of the most disastrous fires that has ever taken place in Inverness. Some tailors had left a fire burning in one of the attics during the night, and in the early morning the whole building was ablaze, including the large shop belonging to Messrs. G. & R. Mackay, several families occupying the upper flats having to make a hasty escape. The site of the fire remained a ruin for some time before the present building, Hamilton Place, was commenced. While excavating at this spot (about twelve feet below the level of the street) the men came on a strata of black earth which had evidently at one time been a peat moss. Further excavations revealed the skeleton of a man and horse, the boots and leather harness being still in fair condition. The remains were supposed to have been that of one of Montrose's troopers who were passing through the town after the Battle of Inverlochy, which took place in 1645.

CHAPTER III.

NEW STREET—ROYAL ACADEMY—CHAPEL OF EASE—DR.
BELL'S INSTITUTION—ROSE STREET—ROSE STREET
FOUNDRY.

WE are still at the top of " New " Street, now Academy
Street. That gentleman who has just passed us is Mr.
Hunter, the genial session-clerk, who is on his way to
his office in Theatre Lane. His duties are not, meantime, of a very onerous nature. Within the Court on
the right hand side of the lane is Edward's Square,
named after Sheriff Edwards. We are now at " the
smiddy," where there is at all times a large array of
horses standing waiting to get shod. Mr. Fraser, the
blacksmith, is, as you will observe, fully occupied. This
establishment is always a rendezvous for those who
desire to impart and receive the latest news, and you
may be sure many interesting subjects are daily dis-
cussed. Adjoining "the smiddy" there are the livery
stables of Mr. Adam Ross, a gentleman whose superior
appearance and genial disposition makes him a general
favourite throughout the surrounding district. That
mansion just below, with the steps leading to the second
floor, is the town house of the Mackintoshes of Aberarder.
Provost Mackintosh sat in the civic chair from 1797
till 1800. This distinguished family was always held
in high esteem among the people of Inverness. The
next building you will notice is one which is somewhat
difficult to describe, insomuch that it has a wing that
extends well·on to the middle of the street, while a

massive stone balustrade leads to the offices beneath. The general outline reminds one of an Italian chateau, does it not? The lower part is occupied by a well-known townsman, Mr. David Prophet, writer. Over the way you will observe standing in his doorway the military figure of Sergeant John Mackenzie, who has had the honour of serving his king and country in many climes. Further down is Ettles Lane. This has been a well-known name in Inverness for many years, the poet Burns, when on his visit to the Highlands, having put up at Ettle's Hotel. That handsome building further down the street is occupied by General Mackenzie, who was connected with the Seaforth Highlanders, being their first colonel. You ask what that high wall is which looks as if it were enclosing a nunnery or the local penitentiary. It is, however, the wall of neither a penitentiary nor a nunnery, but simply that of Raigmore's garden. Inside is the laird's town residence. This street, you will observe, is not paved with granite blocks but with round boulders, there being sufficient earth between each of the stones to produce a luxuriant crop of grass, which, indeed, gives an appearance of rustic beauty to the thoroughfare, and will doubtless prove a tempting morsel to the first flock of sheep that passes. In recent years there has, however, been a vast improvement in the roadways throughout the town, although as yet we are much behind many southern towns in this respect. It is rumoured, however, that ere many years the iron horse, the pioneer of all improvements, will penetrate the utmost recesses of the Highlands, and when it arrives in our midst we may expect to see the roads and pathways of our old town done up like those of other important towns further south, and the architecture of our public buildings up-to-date in every respect, while the grandeur of the surrounding scenery and our historic associations will, doubtless, draw visitors from all parts of the earth. But enough of this ; let us proceed.

We will now enter the Royal Academy Park. These young people you see romping about are the pupils, it being their noon play hour. You will observe that they seem highly elated to-day, the reason being, as I happen to know, that they have just received a letter from the Marquis of Normandy in acknowledgment of their letter to the young Queen on the occasion of her marriage. The epistle was signed in name of the scholars by Masters A. Penrose Hay and Angus B. Reach. You take my word, many of those bright youths will yet make their mark in their country's history. We will now proceed further down the street. That is the Chapel of Ease with the elms in front of it. It is a plain, unpretentious edifice, pretty much in keeping with the times in which it was erected—1790. It was opened by the Rev. Rowland Hill, the celebrated English preacher and wit. The pulpit was for some time occupied by an ex-army chaplain, the Rev. Lachlan Bain, who served in Egypt with Sir Ralph Abercrombie. We are now turning into Margaret Street. On the right is the site, until lately, of the Roman Catholic Chapel. That building you observe in course of erection in Farraline Park is Dr. Bell's Institution. The beautiful Grecian portico with magnificently carved laurel wreaths is from designs by the Clerk of Works, Mr. Henry Burrell. Mr. John Hendrie is foreman mason. The school bids fair to be a great acquisition to the educational interests of the town. The magnificent stretch of ground at the back and front of the building cannot fail to be amply appreciated as a recreation ground by the scholars. Retracing our steps, we now reach New

Street (Academy Street) again. On the opposite side is
the establishment of Messrs. Black & Sons, plumbers,
which is perhaps the oldest established business of the
kind in the north of Scotland, having been opened in
1802 as a branch establishment from Messrs. Marshall,
of Edinburgh. We have now reached School Lane, and
we will again cross to the right side of the street. That
house (now Mitchell's Hotel) has been for many years
the residence of Simon Fraser of Lovat. We are now at
Harold's Court, so named after that genial old Waterloo
hero, Mr. Harold Chisholm, who is standing at the
entrance smoking the pipe of peace after his many
fights up and down through the Peninsula. When in
the humour Harold can tell many strange and stirring
tales of desperate encounters, hairbreadth escapes, and
terrible privations during this great contest. He is, as
you will perceive, every inch a soldier, one of the good
old school, and did time permit we might with profit
enter into conversation with him, for there are few
men living who can give a more vivid description of
the great struggle of the 18th of June 1815, when the
hopes and ambitions of the Little Corporal were for
ever shattered. On some other occasion we may have
a chat with the old soldier. You will observe that there
is a little more bustle at this point, the cause being that
"Bobby All" is coming up the street in a state of
inebriation, and is quarrelling with all and sundry. We
have now turned into Rose Street. At the entrance to
the foundry you will notice the men placing a very
large fly-wheel on a huge truck. This is part of an
engine with which it is proposed to work lead mines
on the hill beyond Beaufort Castle. Whether the
venture will prove a success is another question. For
my own part I am somewhat doubtful, but there is no
proof like a trial, or, as they say in the doric, " the

proof o' the puddin' is the preein' o't." Mr. Smith is
busy superintending the loading operations, and that
workman taking a leading part is Mr. Maclachlan,
blacksmith. Beyond the foundry you will notice a
mansion-house with two poplar trees on either side of
the entrance, while on the other side are the residences
of many well-to-do citizens, prominent among whom is
Captain Fraser of Knockie. . Further on is the house of
Mr. Macpherson, father of Mr. Macpherson, solicitor.
We will retrace our steps, and on a future occasion will
continue our observations.

NOTE.—Dr. Andrew Bell was born at St. Andrews in
1753, and was educated at the University of that place.
Subsequently taking orders in the Church of England,
he was appointed one of the chaplains at Fort St.
George, Madras. While there he was entrusted by the
directors of the East India Company with the management of an institution for the education of the orphan
children of the European military. From this point he
took a life-long interest in the education of the children
of the poor, both at home and in the colonies. His
efforts produced a lasting influence on the educational
interests of this country. Later in life he was made a
prebendary of Westminster, also a member of various
learned societies. He died in 1832, leaving (besides a
valuable estate) £120,000 of 3 per cent. stocks for the
purpose of founding various educational institutions in
seven cities and towns in Scotland, including Inverness,
hence the erection of Bell's School in Farraline Park at
this time. If we mistake not the Merkinch and Central
Schools also received some pecuniary benefit from Dr.
Bell's Trust. The foreman mason alluded to was the
late Mr. John Hendrie of Castleheather, who subsequently undertook and carried out with marked success·

many large contracts in and around Inverness. The surveyor of works, Mr. Henry Burrell, was father of our esteemed townsman, Mr. W. J. M. Burrell, collector, Clachnaharry. Mr. Harold Chisholm, referred to in the foregoing, was present with his regiment, the 92nd, at the battle of Waterloo. After taking their position on the field to await the attack of the enemy, an officer of Cuirassiers was seen to approach in too close proximity to the Highlanders' position, and seemed in no hurry to get away. The commanding officer quietly asked if any of the men could help to unhorse the arrogant Frenchman. Harold stepped out of the ranks, took aim, and a few minutes later the officer was borne to the rear a prisoner. At a cattle show dinner, held in Bell's Park in 1845, an officer who was present referred to the incident, and was not a little surprised when told that Chisholm lived within a short distance from where he stood. "And," replied the officer, "has anything special been done for him?" Some short time thereafter Harold had the satisfaction of receiving a substantial addition to his pension.

CHAPTER IV.

THE LONGMAN ROAD—NEW STREET—THE GAS WORKS—
CHAPEL STREET—CHAPELYARD BURYING-GROUND.

IT is with pleasure that we again resume our pere-
grinations, while we find ourselves at the east end of
Rose Street, and, in order to enjoy the summer breeze,
let us continue our way eastward on to the Longman
Road, which lies between two old stone dykes, shaded
by a rough hedging, a veritable haunt of stoats, weasels,
and such like vermin. To the right is the small farmhouse of Seafield, tenanted by Mr. Ross, while to the
left are the lands of Needlefield and Cromwell's Fort.
Further on to the left is an unpretentious building,
surrounded by a high wall. This is the powder
magazine, where the extra stores of powder required in
connection with the burgh are kept. It was erected
after the terrible gunpowder explosion which took place
in the Black Vennel in 1805. We have now reached
the Longman, as the foreshore is called. How it came
to be designated " the Longman," or " the Longman's
Grave," rather, is not precisely recorded. It has, however, been suggested that the reason for it being so
called was that at one time it was a favourite place for
the landing of contraband goods, and that as a signal
for the coast being clear for that purpose, the receivers
on shore were wont to elevate a figure on a pole as a
sign to the smuggling crews that the coast was clear,
and that operations might begin. A few yards to the east
of the roadway here, the three executions which took

place during the last century were carried out, the last victim of the gallows at this point being John Adams, who was hung for the murder of his wife at "the Mulbuie."

We will now return townwards. These two well-to-do-looking gentlemen who are just coming towards us are Provost Cumming and Captain Godsman, who are taking their afternoon constitutional. We are now nearing the west end of Rose Street. That peculiar looking customer in front of us is John Fraser ("Jock Loch na Shannish"), clad in broad "Kilmarnock bonnet," blue swallow-tail coat, with brass buttons, and corduroy trousers. He is accompanied by his wife, Betty, wearing her conventional shawl and clean white cap. They are out for a holiday, and as John's partiality for his native beverage, "mountain dew," is well known, we sincerely hope that he may return as steady on his legs as we see him now. We are once again on New Street. That building, roofed with red tiles, almost directly opposite, was erected about the year 1782 as a Wesleyan Chapel. Next door is the residence of a well-known local ironfounder. On the door there you will observe the legend "Smith," which is sufficient to indicate that he is, if not the chief, at least a member of the strongest clan in existence. Directly opposite is the wholesale and retail spirit warehouse of Mr. Hogg, while over-head is Lyon's Hall, the only place in town for public entertainments, with the exception of the Northern Meeting Rooms. The building next door is occupied by the Misses Lyon, sisters of Bailie Lyon, a well-known public man, and father of Provost Colin Lyon Mackenzie. We are now at the head of what is known as the Kiln Close, and a little further on there, to the right, is Gas Lane, leading up to the Gasworks. We may just as well take a stroll through the works.

That genial-looking gentleman you see standing at the
gate is Mr. Esson, the manager, who, in addition to being
an expert at the manufacture of gas, has the reputation
of being a remarkably clever bone-setter (in fact, the
only one in town) as well as an excellent dentist.

You may, perhaps, be interested to know that the
Gasworks were opened in September 1827 by the
Inverness Gas and Water Company, and have ever since
been considered an enormous boon to the town. It is
certainly a great advance as compared with the old style,
but I should not be at all surprised to hear of even it
being improved on by some future inventive genius.
Previous to the advent of gas, the town was only dimly
lighted, train-oil lamps being set on the top of poles,
while here and there an iron bracket, to which a lamp
was suspended, might be seen projecting from the gable
of a house or at the end of a close or court. When
nightfall set in, the lamplighter, bearing a torch and
ladder, might be seen wending his way through muddy
streets, followed by a group of urchins calling out, " Looly,
looly, light the lamp." Time will not permit us meantime to inspect the works, otherwise we might ask a
permit from Mr. Esson. This we may, however, do on
a future occasion, when we will doubtless get many eye
openers, and discover something of the manufacture of
this marvellous lighting power.

We now leave the Gasworks and Gas Lane behind,
and find ourselves in Chapel Street. That old lady you
observe coming up the street, who seems to be in need of
protection, is Nanny Do Dolan. She is in her usual state
of inebriation, and you will observe that she is followed
by a large crowd of youngsters, who are bent on giving
her every possible annoyance. Let us look forward
hopefully to the time when such creatures will be better
protected, and more tenderly dealt with. On the right,

beyond that group of thatched cottages, is the gate of
the Chapelyard, and see, there is the kind-hearted and
obliging sexton, Mr. John Martin, who is ever willing
and desirous to assist and help the poor with whom he
comes in contact in the course of his official duties. Mr.
Martin is a staunch temperance man, and has just become an office-bearer in the Clachnacuddin Tent of
Rechabites, recently formed in town by Dr. Macmillan
and Mr. Troup, two of the travelling delegates of the
Order. We will now enter the gate of the burying-
ground. In front of us there, in the direction of the
Gasworks, there stood a small pre-Reformation Chapel,
hence the name Chapelyard. The ground was presented to the town by Margaret Cuthbert, one of the
Cuthberts of Castlehill, about the year 1680. The
generous donor subsequently married a Fraser. Her
last resting-place may be observed on the pathway leading north, parallel with the boundary wall to the right,
a simple slab, bearing her name and the date of her
death, 1714. Perhaps it may occur to some future
generation to place a more imposing memorial over the
grave of this generous lady. There are, as you will
observe, several enclosures, and these mark the burial
places of such families as Macleod of Macleod, Forbes
of Culloden, and many others connected with the Highlands and notable in Scottish history, while nearer the
street wall is interred a bishop and dean of the Scottish
Episcopal Church, and an officer who was mortally
wounded at Culloden, Captain Joseph Jackson of
Carlisle. The high wall, you will notice, is strongly
suggestive of resurrection times. That fine row of
poplars you see skirting the wall is much admired by
visitors. We now find ourselves on the street, and as
it is time to return home for the day, we will resume
our observations on a future date.

Note.—The powder magazine, or powder house as it used to be called, was removed to the east end of the Longman Road shortly after the explosion in 1805 of the former powder store, which was situated in Baron Taylor's Lane, on or near the site of Mr. Grant's meal store. The accident alluded to took place in this wise. The powder was stored in rooms on the first floor, while the ground floor was used as a candle work. The man in charge accepted an invitation from a friend to go out and have a dram, and remaining rather long, the tallow in the boiler took fire, the flames speedily reaching the next floor, a terrific explosion ensued. A young lady belonging to a much respected family in town was passing through a close just in front of Mrs. Logan's pianoforte establishment, and was at once struck down. A group of persons gathered round the prostrate lady, and some of the group asked who she was. The lady replied, "I am Miss Fraser of Farraline," and almost instantly expired. A woman passing with a baby in her arms at the top of Bank Lane had her fingers blown off, while the baby was killed. The writer's grandmother, who was in domestic service with a Miss Grant, who boarded officers stationed in the town, was standing at the top of a close below the Caledonian Hotel after bringing up stoups of water from the river. The explosion was heard all over the town, while much damage was done to windows in the immediate vicinity. It does seem strange that the authorities (if there were such) should allow candle works to be carried on under a powder store. Verily, the arrangements offered a premium to disaster. The entry still known as the Kiln Close, situated at the foot of Academy Street, led to a number of erections known at the time as kilns. The farmers and crofters about the town used to send their supplies of barley to get dried and converted into malt wherewith to make ale, which was at this time used as a staple article of food. After the passing of the Bill in 1760 imposing a tax on malt the buildings fell into disuse. In 1770 one of the old kilns was rented by the Methodist Society as a preaching place. There is a document extant which sets forth, "That for the sum of four pounds a year John Mackay agrees to clean the kiln and keep the boys away from the door." Truly the boys have been much the same in all ages. In 1777 the first regular Methodist preacher was appointed to Inverness, Rev. Duncan MacCallum, whose name appears on the Society books until well on in the nineteenth century. He was apparently the Methodist "Apostle of the North." His only daughter married a Mr. Morley of Newcastle, who subsequently became grandfather of Mr. John Morley, M.P. The building on Academy Street, nearly opposite Rose Street referred to, was subsequently rented by the Methodists as a meeting place till 1797. It is recorded that here John Wesley, the great evangelist and founder of Methodism, preached on a Monday evening at seven o'clock, on Tuesday morning at five, and again in the evening. This took place in May 1784.

CHAPTER V.

CHAPEL   STREET   (*continued*) — GREYFRIARS'   BURYING-
GROUND — FRIARS'   STREET — FACTORY   STREET —
MAGGOT—WATERLOO PLACE—JOHN ORDE'S CIRCUS.

WE will now resume our journey where we discon-
tinued it on Chapel Street, and let us proceed down
town.   Almost directly opposite the Chapelyard Gate is
North Church Lane.   That stern, military-looking man,
with clean-shaven face and conventional silk hat, is
Mr. William Clunas, another Waterloo hero, who endured much hardship and privation with his regiment,
the 92nd Highlanders, throughout the Peninsular War,
and at the great final struggle outside Brussels.   We
will step across and converse with him for a few
minutes, as he is ever willing to relate his adventures
and fight his battles over again.   Now that you have
spoken to him, don't you think him a most interesting
old gentleman?   These yarns of his all bear the hall-
mark of truth.   He is at present engaged in the coal
trade, and is altogether a most industrious and prosperous citizen.   We will now turn into North Church
Place, where we pass the residence of Mr. Clunas.
That sacred edifice in front is the recently erected
North Church, principally intended for the Gaelic-
speaking people of the district.   The pastor is the Rev.
Archibald Cook, a divine of the good old school, who is
noted for his quaint sayings.   He is much respected by
his people, in whom he takes a deep interest.   We are
now on Friars' Street.   This part of the town, from the

northern boundary of the High Churchyard, was formerly the glebe land, consisting of six acres, which were set apart for the use of the ministers of the Parish Church (St. Mary's). A little to the south is the Greyfriars' Churchyard. Near the entrance gate there you will observe a solitary pillar, which is the only remaining vestige of the old Greyfriars' Priory. It has been for centuries consecrated as a burial place for the Baillies and Macleans resident in the district, although other families have from time to time been privileged to bury their dead there. There are, as you will observe, within its gates several monuments of more than ordinary interest, prominent among which is that much-disfigured effigy of what is supposed to be the Earl of Mar, who was Governor of Inverness early in the fourteenth century. The street names in this locality indicate that it was the happy hunting-ground of the "Friars of Orders Grey" in pre-Reformation times. We have no doubt that many a plump salmon was caught by them in the silvery waters of the Ness at that point now known as Friars' Shott. We will turn northward. Over the way is Mr. Frank Fraser's brewery, where he turns out an article which is much appreciated by his patrons, although the habit of ale consumption is not now so prevalent in Inverness as it was in former years, when it used to be taken by the working-class as "kitchen" to their porridge. We have now reached the north end of Friars' Street, and that block of buildings which you observe on the left, with the lime trees in front, is the canvas and sail factory belonging to Messrs. Mackintosh. They still employ a goodly number of hands, but the trade is, I regret to say, considerably on the decline, owing to the competition of the Dundee manufacturers. You ask what that unusual tinkling sound is. That is the music with which old

Donald Fraser, the bellman, regales the ears of the
citizens. See, there he is turning the corner. The
funeral of one of the humbler classes is about to take
place, and this is the way in which the public are
invited. Let us follow him. You will observe people
are gathering from every direction. We have now
reached the door of the house of mourning, and you
will observe the "bearer" (bier) leaning against the
doorway. According to custom it was placed there
early in the morning by the sexton as an indication
that the funeral would take place during the day. A
few paces more and we are in Factory Street. It has
derived its name from being the place of residence of
the workmen employed in the several factories in the
district. This is the district known as "the Maggot."
Many have some difficulty in arriving at the derivation
of the name, which can scarcely be called a savoury
one. It has recently been authenticated that it is
simply a corruption of the name St. Margaret, the
saintly wife of our Scottish King Malcolm Canmore,
and daughter of Edward the Confessor. This is only
another instance of how names become corrupted, and I
see no good reason why the authorities should not
revert to the historical name. The place is the residence of a number of respectable working people,
although now that work in the factories is getting
scarce, and poverty becoming more pronounced, it is
getting somewhat into disrepute. Facing the river
you will observe that small unpretentious building;
it is the schoolhouse, presided over by Mr. Duncan
Mackay, familiarly known as "Cripple Dunk." Let us
have a peep in at the window. See, there is Mr.
Mackay industriously teaching his pupils. Among
them are some intelligent lads, who, although of humble
parentage, may yet be heard of. The penny a week is

saved by the parents out of their scanty earnings to enable the young people to take their place in the great struggle for existence. There is no supervisory board over Dunk, and yet he is as careful in moulding the characters of his pupils as if directly under the eye of distinguished educationists. Let us now move down to Waterloo Place, which was formerly known as Wellington Street, but, possibly in honour of the many Waterloo veterans in town, the name has been changed. There are, you will notice, some comfortable residences here, and one or two inns or taverns. Over to the right is the large space known as the Maggot Green. You will observe a small booth there and several of the equine tribe around it. The younger people are gathering around muchly interested. That tall, kindly-looking old fellow you see patting one of the horses is John Orde, the famous equestrian, while that young, active-looking chap by his side is Delaney. They have just arrived in town. They are well known all over Scotland, and as their performances are all in the open air, they never fail to draw a large concourse of spectators. There will be two gold watches, three silver ones, a boll of meal, and a young pig raffled for after the performance. The crowd is now growing in immensity, and the performance is just about to begin. Mr. Orde announces that there will be an indoor performance in Lyon's Hall in the evening, when the play will be the ever-green Scotch drama of "Wandering Steenie." By the tardy use of the whip the ring is enlarged, and see how the sale of raffle tickets goes on. That is the stage manager, Mr. Fisher, who is exhibiting the gold watches on the end of the stick, while his assistants are also displaying sundry articles which are also to be sacrificed. Let us hope that the opening scene may be "Dick Turpin's Ride to York." We are disappointed.

See, it is "Billy Button, the Tailor's Equestrian Adventures," we are going to witness. The younger members of the troupe are exceedingly smart, aren't they? their tumbling performance being excellent. All eyes, however, are turned on the veteran, who just makes his appearance. There he is dressed as an old farmer, and he has, apparently great difficulty in mounting his favourite horse, "Cromarty." He has now succeeded, you will observe, and has become marvellously expert. Look, he has even managed to get to his feet on the saddle, while "Cromarty," at a brisk pace, canters round the ring to a lively tune played by the entire orchestra, consisting of a fiddle and trombone. Now, off goes the farmer's togs, and we see a jolly jack tar, then a drunken hussar, and anon, a Newhaven fishwife, all equally expert equestrians. Now he has thrown off the fishwife's duds and appears as Rob Roy, the great Scottish freebooter, in which garb he finishes up this part of the performance. The lottery tickets are now pretty well disposed of, and that is Delaney engaged in his famous ladder performance. While the fireworks are being prepared, and before the crowd begins to separate, we will take our departure, resolving on a future occasion to "pull for the shore."

NOTE.—Mr. William Clunas, the Waterloo hero referred to above, was a splendid specimen of the Highland soldier of the days of Wellington. He was brimful of anecdotes concerning the Peninsular campaign, and, like most old soldiers, was in nowise averse to fighting his battles over again. In relating his experiences he was wont to tell how on one occasion the corps to which he belonged ran short of water; by good luck there was a copious supply of wine at hand, which, in addition to being freely partaken of as a beverage, was one day used to boil the potatoes for dinner. At another place, where water seems to have been more abundant, he went out once under a heavy fire to obtain a camp kettle from a well close by the encampment. On his way back, however, a "bullet found its billet" in the utensil, which was in a moment converted into a watering-can, so that when he arrived back among his thirsty comrades he had no sparkling draught from the crystal spring to offer them. Mr. Clunas, as was to be expected, did not go scathless through the campaign, being wounded severely in one engagement. He, however, lived to a good old age, and was much respected in Inverness, where he carried on a lucrative coal business. Mr. Clunas died in 1860.

CHAPTER VI.

SHORE STREET—PORTLAND PLACE—OLD QUAY—THE
LAUNCH—NEW QUAY—LOTLAND PLACE.

As arranged when last we parted, we take as our starting point this morning the junction of Chapel Street
and Glebe Street, and we will continue our walk north-
wards along Shore Street towards the harbour. The
first object of interest we come to is Mr. Anderson's
sawmill, which is situated there. It is, as you will
observe, quite an extensive establishment, and being in
full working order, there are a number of men employed.
The buildings are of a somewhat fragile and flimsy
nature, and would very rapidly be demolished in case
of conflagration. I should be inclined to think that a
shrewd insurance agent who had the interest of his
company at heart would name a very high premium
for such a structure. To the left, and almost directly
opposite, is Winchester's coal yard, where a considerable
supply of salt herrings is regularly kept in stock and
sold in large quantities. Round the corner there may
be seen a block of somewhat pretentious buildings,
known as Portland Place, erected in 1828, and which,
from their style of architecture, would help to adorn a
more aristocratic locality. The row of buildings on the
right here, stretching northward along Shore Street,
reminds me forcibly of a remark once made by a callous
Yankee, who had no love for the antique, while going
through the Forum at Rome, " Splendid buildings, but
sadly out of repair." In front of Portland Place and

running parallel with it is the Old Quay. The tide is just coming in, and that brown-sailed vessel lying berthed is an East Coast herring boat laden down with silvery beauties. She has just arrived, and our old friend Donald Fraser, who is always on the alert with his bell, is, in stentorian voice, announcing to the thrifty housewives in the neighbourhood the fresh supplies, which he tells them are to be retailed at " twenty-six a penny." You will observe they are something like herring, there being nothing of the garvie about them. You ask what that gathering crowd which hurriedly travels shoreward means. Why, can't you see the magnificent display of bunting all around? That means that there are to be no less than two vessels launched at "The Shore" to-day. See with what eager anticipation the school children look forward to the sight as they make their way in the direction of the yards. They have just had their mid-day " play-time " extended an hour, and are hurrying down along with their elders to witness the unique sight. Ladies in their grandest holiday attire, accompanied by male friends, who are privileged to go on board the ships, pass along, while occasionally you may observe a musician with his well-polished instrument making his way towards the different yards, for the vessels are usually launched to the strains of music. We have no tickets of admission, but we will, I think, succeed in getting into the yard of Mr. John Cook, where the magnificent schooner " Augusta " is being launched. Having obtained the necessary permission, we will take up our stand right here at the bow of the vessel, where we will have an opportunity of witnessing the christening ceremony. As this gala day only occurs once in the six months, you will observe the workmen are in a state of great bustle, although there is little excite-

ment, everything being done methodically and in order,
knowing that "time and tide will for no man bide." As
the new vessel has to cross the roadway, you will observe
a trench has been made to enable the vessel to glide
safely through, while the man whose duty it is to watch
the tide is showing signs of its being at its height.
Listen! the band aboard has just struck up the well-
known and appropriate nautical air, "Hearts of Oak."
Everything is now ready. Mr. Cook has got the signal
that the tide is at its height. See! the river looks
smooth as a mirror, and is ready to receive the gallant
ship. That energetic, sturdy-looking mechanic is Tom
Carstairs, the foreman carpenter, while these other two
men by his side are Big John Ross and Little John
Ross, two of his leading hands. The "way." is now
greased, and everything is ready for the launch.
Amidst much shouting and excitement, the wedges are
sent home, and look! the ship begins to move.
That lady you see severing the ribbon attached to the
bottle of wine by which the ship is christened is Mrs.
Lawrence, wife of the popular owner, Mr. James
Lawrence, and the "Augusta" now glides gracefully into
the silvery waters of the Ness. Let us join with the
other spectators in the shout which rends the air.
Now she floats like the swan on the lake, while the
band has changed their tune to "I'm afloat." Doesn't
she look a beauty, and we can only wish Captain
Tolmie, her gallant master, every success with her on
the rolling tide. Preparations are now being made in
the yard for an entertainment to the workmen in the
evening, and you will observe they seem highly elated
in anticipation thereof. Now that we have seen the
launch of the "Augusta," let us have a look at the launch
of that beautiful sloop at Mr. Munro's Yard on the
Capel Inch side of the river. See! she glides into the

water just as gently and smoothly as the "Augusta" did. I tell you these carpenter chaps know their business thoroughly, and are quite as expert as those of the great shipbuilding yards. Indeed, it is said that an Inverness ship carpenter can command a job anywhere; and, judging from their work to-day, I think there is little doubt but that he can hold his own. Having now seen the two launches, we will allow the crowd to disperse, and we will leisurely stroll down as far as the New Quay and have a look at one or two of the vessels berthed there. Both sides of the river, as you will observe, are admirably adapted for launching purposes, the incline being gradual, neither too steep nor too flat. We are now at the New Quay. That nearest schooner is the "Lord Adolphus," which has just arrived from Newcastle with a cargo of coals. The berths are all taken up, you will observe. That vessel getting ready to sail with this tide is the Leith smack "Jean Mackenzie." The "Enterprise" (Paterson, master) is that vessel next her discharging a cargo of lime while alongside her is the smack "Success" (Master John Mackenzie), which has had a somewhat adventurous voyage recently, of which I have no doubt you have heard. There is John himself on deck, apparently not one bit the worse of his tempestuous voyage across the grim and grey North Sea. At this quay most of the vessels lie up from October to March. Over the way is the Ship Inn, and that is the genial tenant, Mr. Tolmie, standing in the doorway. I need hardly say that it is a favourite resort of the mariners of the port, as well as of the ship carpenters belonging to Mr. Cook's yard, and I have no doubt that on pay-nights there are more vessels launched in imagination within its walls than were ever in reality built, while the yarns spun by the sun-browned, weather-beaten

c

bearded seamen in the back room after their return from a voyage will smack of the ozone-laden breeze, and resemble somewhat the tales of Coleridge's "Ancient Mariner," of fearful storms and more fearful calms, when—

> "Down dropt the breeze, the sails dropt down,
> 'Twas sad as sad could be ;
> And all did speak only to break
> The silence of the sea."

That block of buildings a little further on, with steps leading up to them, were originally erected at the beginning of the century as stores for the Inverness Militia, but is now used as a dyeing house for the sail cloth and canvas manufactured at the Sconce. We will turn into Lotland Place, which is chiefly occupied by fishermen belonging to the town who ply their nets in the waters of the Beauly Firth. That small shop with a miscellaneous stock is owned by Mrs. Finlayson, better known, as "Bell Oliver," who is a general favourite in the neighbourhood, and particularly among the youngsters, who delight in her home-made "gundy." We will now cross the Moat Bridge leading into Cromwell's Fort. That gentleman standing in the door of his residence is Mr. Colin Davidson, owner of the schooner "Fowlis" and other vessels. He is, as is his custom, feasting his eyes on that magnificent panoramic view, which is to be got from his garden, of the hills of Wester Ross. We are now on the site of what was once Cromwell's Fort, but as it is now dinner-time, we will retrace our steps homewards, and on another occasion visit this most interesting locality.

NOTE.—Inverness in the past was famed for its shipbuilding. It is somewhere on record that the shipwrights of Inverness received large orders from the

Government of Denmark in the fourteenth century. In 1249 Matthew Prior, the Latin chronicler of the period, describing the armament which accompanied Louis XI., King of France, on his crusading expedition to the Holy Land, speaks of the great ship of the Earl of St. Poll and Blois, a "wonderful vessel," he calls it, which had been built for the Earl at Inverness. No doubt the fine fir forests of Strathglass were used to fulfil these contracts. Mr. John Cook, referred to above, came to Inverness from Aberdeen (of which place he was a native) on "Wild Martinmas" day in 1826. He built many vessels in Inverness, became a member of the Town-Council, and also a Magistrate. With reference to the smack "Success" alluded to, it may be explained that at the time referred to there was considerable talk over an adventurous voyage of this vessel. It appears that Mackenzie, the skipper ("Fruchlain"), had just got his cargo aboard at Peterhead, and left for Inverness, when a terrific gale sprung up, and drove the little vessel across the wild North Sea to Norway. The entire crew was composed of Mackenzie and another seaman. After a few weeks' absence they were taken across to Inverness by some Norwegian pilots, to the relief and joy of their many friends, who had almost given them up for lost. He used to relate that in his hour of danger his only chart was his Bible. Mr. Anderson's sawmill was totally destroyed by fire in the autumn of 1851, being built entirely of wood it offered a premium to disaster.

CHAPTER VII.

CROMWELL'S FORT—THE ROPE AND SAIL WORKS—
COLONEL FITCH'S HOUSE.

WE again find ourselves within the precincts of
Cromwell's Fort, now known as "The Sconce," which
literally means a small fortification or redoubt. It is
altogether a pleasant place, the green sward being both
refreshing and pleasing to the eye. Around us is a
veritable hive of industry—an up-to-date sail and rope
factory, presided over by the genial proprietor, Mr.
Mackintosh, who is one of the most energetic men in
the north. If Invernessians of the future exhibit the
same energy and industry as those of to-day, it will not
be at all surprising if this locality turns out one of the
most flourishing centres of industry in the north. It
has, as you will observe, every advantage, being contiguous
to the harbour, which is capable of being made navigable
for heavy draught vessels. If the landscape all round
is not studded with thriving factories fifty or sixty years
hence, it will be because the wheel of progress has
stopped short. We will first enter the sailmaking department of the factory and have a chat with Mr. Junor,
the overseer of that particular branch of the establishment. He is a most intelligent man, isn't he? and is,
I understand, his employer's right-hand man, much of
the business of the establishment being carried on by
him. The men are busily at work, you will observe,
and the discordant sound of the looms remind us of the

great factories further south. These two men you observe by their looms are Andrew Fraser and J. Cameron, two of the most expert sailmakers in the north. They go about their work, as you will observe, with machine-like regularity, and by them many a young sailmaker has been taught the trade. These girls you see are busily engaged filling pirns for the weavers, and they seem to be adepts at the business, judging from the deft manner in which they go about their work, reminding us of the adage of the wise man, "In all labour there is profit." As you will see from the piles of work before them at present there is a rush on, and some heavy orders are being executed. We will now pass along to the ropemaking department, which is under the supervision of Mr. Duncan Maclennan, who is assisted by Mr. John Campbell ("Voiach"). There is a large staff of workmen, including a number of boys, and they are busily engaged in the somewhat arduous task of rope-spinning. The boys, as you will notice, seem to be as expert as the adults. All kinds of "rope" are manufactured here, from fine twine up to the stoutest cable necessary for mooring purposes. There are generally about ninety hands employed in the factory, while the average earnings of the journeymen range from 12s. to 14s. per week, the boys getting 2s., but by dint of sheer industry and considerable overtime they sometimes succeed in earning 2s. 6d., while the girls have to be satisfied with less. The hours are sixty per week—ten hours a day. Possibly some of the more sanguine of the workmen in their fondest dreams look forward to the passing of something in the shape of a Factory Act that will in some measure ameliorate the present condition of things. They are, however, on the whole a contented lot of workpeople, and the treatment they receive at the hands of the employer compares

favourably with any other establishment of its kind in
the country. Having now seen all that is worth inspecting in the interior of the weaving and spinning sheds,
we will pass out into the open, and will next visit the
famous clock tower. The structure is somewhat primitive. We will now enter it, and ascend to the clock
and have a look at the works, which are of very crude
and ancient construction. Watch your feet on the stair,
and keep a good hold of that rope as you make your
ascent, in case you may get a sudden drop, as, owing to
the lapse of time, these steps are not just as reliable as
they were in the days of Cromwell. We have now
succeeded in gaining the top and can examine the clock
at leisure. It is perhaps one of the oldest clocks in the
country, and at one time adorned the tower of Fortrose
Cathedral, from whence it was removed to its present
position by Cromwell's Ironsides. You will therefore
see that it has a strange and varied history. At one
time it sounded the sweet matins and vespers, tolling
the sweet hour of prayer, at another announcing the
hour of relief to Cromwell's several guards, and later
on, indicating to the industrious denizens of The Sconce
when to resume and cease their daily toil. From the
appearance of the old clock one would almost think that,
like Tennyson's "Brook," it seems to say—

"Men may come and men may go,
　But I go on for ever."

We will now descend and take a look round the
Ramparts. The tide being in, the Fort, as you will
observe, is to a great extent surrounded by water. See
these youngsters how they seem to enjoy bathing in the
moats. Many an expert local swimmer made his first
acquaintance with the water at this point. We will
now retrace our steps and have a look at this vessel
which is making her way up the river. She is the

"Ocean Wave," with a cargo of raw material from Archangel for manufacture at The Sconce. By the way, I might mention that that house, which, as I said on our last visit, is the residence of Mr. Colin Davidson, was originally the residence of Colonel Fitch, the governor of the Citadel during its brief occupation. We will now cross the moat bridge, and we find ourselves once more on Shore Street. We have no time to go over the shipping in the harbour again, but you will notice that it is quite as busy as on our previous visit to this locality. See! there is the crew of a newly-moored schooner making for the Ship Inn, there to satisfy something like three or four days' thirst, for they most likely haven't tasted a drop since they set sail from Newcastle. Although only a few days have elapsed since our last visit, see, they are already laying the keel of another vessel in Mr. Cook's shipyard. As the day is advancing we had better not linger any longer over these scenes, interesting as they may be. We will, however, continue our exploration on a future occasion, and, if you have no objection, we will select that interesting locality on the opposite side of the river known as the Merkinch, which is, I may mention, the residential district of the seafaring class belonging to the port.

NOTE.—On the advent of the Commonwealth the Highlanders in many instances submitted themselves to the Englishmen without resistance. The soldiers treating the people kindly, abstained from plundering, paying for whatever supplies they received, and generally exercising a civilising influence on the inhabitants. In November 1651 Colonel Fitch occupied Inverness, quartering his men in the Castle and great houses betwixt Spey and Loch Ness. In the spring of the next year he commenced building a citadel, which was to

accommodate 2000 men, horse and foot.   The minister of
Kirkhill (the Rev. James Fraser), writing in his diary
under date 1655, says—"The Citadel of Inverness is
now on a great length, almost finished.   They had first
built a long row of buildings made of bricks and planks
upon the river side to accommodate the regiment, and
ramparts and bulwarks of earth in every street of the
town, and also fortified the Castle and the bridge and
the main court of guard at the Cross."   It is evident
that the promoters of the Commonwealth were in favour
with the Magistrates and other authorities, for, continues
the same writer, " they bought a large plot of land from
the burghers, called Carseland, where they built the
Citadel, founded May 16th, 1652, and now finished, a
most stately scene !   It was five cornered, with bastions,
with a wide trench that an ordinary barque might sail
in at full tide; the breastwork, three storeys, built all of
hewn stone lined within, and a brick wall, sentinel houses
of stone at each corner, a sally to the south leading to
the town, and on the north a great gate called the Port,
with a strong drawbridge of oak called the Blue Bridge,
and a stately structure over the gate well cut with the
Commonwealth arms and the motto, 'Togam turntur
arma.'   This bridge was drawn every night, and a strong
guard within, small schooners and sloops sailing in or
out, the bridge was heaved to give way.   The entry from
the bridge into the Citadel was a stately vault about 70
feet long, with seats on each side, and a row of iron
hooks for pikes and drums to hang on.   In the centre
of the Citadel stood a great four-square building all of
hewn stone, called the magazine and granary.   In the
third storey was the Church, well finished, with a stately
pulpit and seats, a wide bartizan on top, and a brave
great clock, with four large gilded dials and a curious
bell.   North-west and north-east are lower storeys for

ammunition, timber, lodgings for manufacturers, stabl-
ings, provision and brewing houses, and a great long tavern,
in which all manner of viands were sold by one Mr.
Benson, so that the whole regiment was accommodated
within these walls. All their oak planks and beams
were carried out of England in ships to Kessock Roads ;
all their fir logs and spars were sold out of Hugh Fraser
Struy's woods. I saw that gentleman receive 30,000
merks at once for timber. Most of their best hewn
stone was taken from Chanonry, great Cathedral and
Steeple and Bishop's Castle was razed, also the Church
and Abbey of Kinloss and Beauly, the Greyfriar's and St.
Mary's Chapel at Inverness, and many more, the whole
cost amounting to about £80,000." It must have been
a brave structure, calculated to overawe the neighbouring
clans as it stood there strong and impregnable with its
blue banner floating above with the name "Emmanuel"
written upon it in letters of gold. But this state of
affairs was not destined to last long, for nine years later,
on the restoration of Charles II., the fortress was
demolished by the infuriated Highlanders amidst considerable hilarity. Subsequently the English troops left
the town with much regret. A few of them, however,
settled in the town, where their descendants still remain.
"Never people left a place," says the minister, "with
such reluctance. It was sad to see and hear their sighs
and tears, pale faces and embraces at their parting fare-
well from that town, and no wonder, they had peace
and plenty for ten years in it ; they made that place
happy, and it made them so. The Citadel was slighted
and the country called in to raze it. I saw it founded ;
I saw it flourish ; I saw it in its glory and grandeur,
and now in its ruins. 'Sic transit gloria mundi.'"
According to Dr. Johnson, the soldiers of Cromwell
first taught the people of Inverness to make shoes and

plant kail, and to speak the English language with
elegance. What a different state of matters the foregoing presents to that which the Stuarts were wont to
exercise towards the luckless Highlanders to whom they
showed such inane devotion! When they came to the
north they exercised their prerogative by hanging off a
few Highland chiefs simply to evince their power.
Perhaps the act by which they are known best is that
of granting to the town the authority of levying the petty
customs, which has been a bone of contention for
centuries. After the battle of Culloden the Duke of
Cumberland conceived the idea of rebuilding Cromwell's
Fort, the chief feature of which was that the main street
in the town should be made in a straight line from the
southern or principal gate to the Cross, so that in the
event of a disturbance arising from any cause whatever,
the street could easily be swept with cannon from the
gate of the proposed citadel, but the town authorities,
who were no favourities with "The Butcher," put serious
obstacles in the way of his doing so, which gave him
great offence. An incident which took place the day
after Culloden may here be related incidentally. When
Provost Hossack of Inverness waited upon the Duke at
his hotel (probably "The Horns" at the top of Bridge
Street) with a view to request him to be more lenient
in his treatment of the Highlanders, General Hawley,
the hero of Falkirk (?), stepped forward and kicked the
worthy Provost down the stair, saying, "How dare you
dictate to us, you impudent puppy?" At the refusal of
the town authorities to accede to the Duke's request
with regard to the Citadel, the Marquis of Huntly
offered that promontory opposite Chanonry to the
Government. It was ordered to be surveyed, pronounced suitable, and orders were given for the construction of Fort-George, which was commenced under

the superintendence of General Skinner. It was completed in twelve years at the cost of £160,000. It may be easily conceived what fear the Government of that day had for the Highlanders when they thought it necessary to so overawe them by placing such a strong fortress in their midst. At the time of the building of the Fort the farm servants in the county stipulated with their masters that they should be allowed a certain part of the year to go and labour at the Fort, where they received from 6d. to 8d. per day, which we have no doubt was made good use of by them, the building of the Fort thus becoming to them a veritable blessing in disguise. We may further state that it was at this time that ploughmen in the district had their wages increased to £1 in the half-year, including their meal, milk, &c.

CHAPTER VIII.

THE BLACK BRIDGE—ANDERSON STREET—GRANT STREET—
PUMPGATE STREET—LOWER KESSOCK STREET.

BEFORE we cross over to the Merkinch side of the river
to-day, let us take a parting glance at Shore Street. If
you have no objection we will again retrace our steps a
short distance in that direction. That gentleman you
observe standing in the door of the Custom House is
Mr. Hood, the collector, whose portly figure is a
familiar one in the vicinity. He is an able and efficient officer, and discharges his arduous and delicate
duties in a manner which gain him much popularity.
In addition to his ordinary staff he has frequently to
employ extra hands to remain with the ships while in
port to see that no contraband goods are landed without the necessary tariff being imposed. That gentleman,
who has just bade us "Guid mornin'" in his homely
doric, is Mr. Johnstone, skinner, who is always at the
head of his business, and is considered one of our most
industrious business men. We will now return with a
view to crossing over the Black Bridge to the Merkinch.
Having now traversed Portland Place, we are at what
is known as the "Lazy Corner." On our left there at
the "black shed" is a group of harbour hangers-on.
They usually wait "arrivals" here, and between their
expectorations discuss subjects, sometimes grave, sometimes gay, but not always edifying. See, there is something or somebody attracting their attention just now,
judging from the hearty manner in which they seem to

THE BLACK BRIDGE.

be enjoying themselves. Let us have a look. Oh, yes, it is Dola Young, an inoffensive local character, who forms the centre of the group, and is giving them a terpsichorean exhibition to the extemporised music of one of the bystanders. However amusing such a performance may be, it would suit these able-bodied fellows much better if they were otherwise employed. They get into the habit of standing at this corner, and it seems to be a kind of second nature to them. In fact many of them may be seen there from daylight to dark, and in their regularity are examples to those better employed. Dola's performance is now over, and he will consider himself amply paid if he gets one of the smallest coins of the realm or a chew of tobacco. See, he has just obtained the latter, and with swinging step goes on his way rejoicing up Waterloo Place. He will doubtless be waylaid by another group before he goes much further. We are now on the Wooden or Black Bridge, which, although by no means an ornament, yet no one can gainsay its utility. It was erected in 1809, the fir woods of Strathglass being taxed for the supply of its beams, &c. It cost about £2000, much of which was contributed by private subscription by the neighbouring proprietors. Down till 1836 a toll of ½d. on each passenger was levied to assist in paying the interest of the cost yet unpaid. That peculiar-looking character coming along townwards is a member of the ubiquitous Clan Fraser, but is popularly known by the less romantic name "Macgitten." The flock of pigs which gruntingly hobble along in front of him, he is just bringing over from the Black Isle, where he has purchased them. From his appearance one would scarcely take him for a pig drover. The tall hat and frock coat give him somewhat of a clerical look, which is certainly not the general aspect of a dealer in live

stock. You will observe that he seems to be on familiar
terms with his flock, and Father-o'-Flynn-like "helping
the lazy ones on with a stick." He does not seem,
however, in the best of humour at present, so far as we
can observe. The reason is not far to seek; he is
after having a somewhat noisy altercation with Hector
Mackenzie, the collector of petty customs at the toll
box yonder, but had ultimately to yield to the old
Seaforth veteran, who manages to collect every fraction
of dues without the aid of gate or barrier of any kind.
As compensation for his annoyance Mr. Fraser feels
assured that the few butchers who are in town will
purchase his stock-in-trade at a profit, and enable him
to make another venture into the country. He will
doubtless have a glass or two in the Plough Inn this
evening, when all his anger will have vanished. Hector,
who has seen much service with his regiment, including the battle of Maida in 1809, has done sentry go at
this point for many years. By a strange coincidence
the collector at the upper bridge is a namesake, and
also a Seaforth Highlander, but more of him anon. On
the right hand side there, at the corner of Anderson
Street and Grant Street, is Luckie Cameron's public-
house, at the door of which you will observe a group of
typical Merkinch sailors, among them being Angus
Mackenzie ("Big Angus"), John Mackenzie ("Barney"),
James Fraser ("Jimmie Lachlan"), Donald Stewart
("Sporran"), John Chisholm ("Smiddy"), John Fraser
("Trumpet"), and John Fraser ("Black Jock"), the latter
of whom has just returned from a foreign voyage, and is
spinning his yarns with much apparent good humour.
His listeners have all sailed the same seas, and are
much interested. There is another group standing in
front of Rory Maclennan's ("Hovack") pie shop, among
whom is Sandy Macdonald, the printer, whose father is

owner of the smack "Recovery." He is, as you can gather from the conversation, engaged in a heated debate with Kenny Mackenzie ("A'things") over the sailing properties of the "Recovery" and the "Success," the latter of which outsailed his father's vessel coming up the Firth last week with a fair wind. The company is now about to adjourn to Ali the Blanket's public-house, where the discussion will doubtless be continued o'er "a wee drappie o't." Over the way is the Star Inn, the favourite hostelry of our old favourite, Mr. Orde, when he comes to town. We are now at Murdo Maclennan's ("Buie") smiddy. See, there he stands in the doorway, a veritable son of Vulcan, with his sleeves rolled up, displaying "the muscles of his brawny arms, strong as iron bands." By his side is Norman Macleod, skipper of the revenue cutter "Atalanta," which at present is in the Canal Basin. That peculiar-looking customer sitting on the doorstep a little further along is Danie Boatie, who is practising the flute in order to play at the raffle of the model of the brig "Saucy Jean," which is to take place this evening. That was Andrew Fraser ("Abriachan"), carter, who just saluted us, while along there a small distance is that genial old gentleman, Donald Ferguson, sitting at his doorway enjoying the afternoon sunshine. He is the father of the well-known local medical practitioner, Dr. Ferguson. That gentleman to whom he is talking is Mr. Macpherson ("Pony"), innkeeper. The party who has just turned into Grant Street from North Kessock Street is Mr. Maclennan, Whitehouse, the much respected secretary of the Fishermen's and Mariners' Society. We are now on Pumpgate Street, which has derived its name from that pump which you see on the middle of the street, around which a group of women are discussing the latest domestic intelligence. As Telford Street is

the only street of interest beyond, we will retrace our
steps, and now find ourselves in Lower Kessock Street.
There on the right is the Deer's Head Inn, indicating
that its proprietor is of the Caberfeidh—Mackenzie
—Clan. Further on to the right is the smithy, stores,
and office of Messrs. M'Allan Brothers, where a great
amount of work is turned out in connection with shipping. From the amount of work turned out of the
workshop it is worthy of a more dignified name than
" the smiddy," but it seems to suit the purpose quite
well. The Messrs. M'Allan are owners of several
vessels belonging to the port, and do an extensive
general business locally. That is Mr. John M'Allan,
the senior partner, who is standing at the gate in conversation with one of his skippers, Mr. James Gray,
who has charge of the schooner "Laverock." Messrs.
M'Allan are justly proud of having in their employment
such a fine old type of salt as Skipper Gray. Let us
have a talk with Mr. M'Allan. Now that we have con-
versed with him, you will doubtless have observed from
his grasp of Parliamentary affairs, upon which he is
ever eager to speak, that he is a politician of more than
ordinary intelligence, and a staunch sound Liberal at
that. The three brothers are known throughout the
locality for their charity and philanthropy, being ever
ready with their means and advice in assisting the
deserving poor, as we ourselves can amply testify. On
the opposite side of the street is the residence of Mr.
Lawrence, shipowner, to whom we have already referred.
We will continue our way northward towards the White
House, the residence of Mr. Maclennan. What means
this apparition on the roadway in front? Can it be a
moving whin bush, or is it a " Jack in the green ?"
No, it is none other than that strange and eccentric
character " Fearrachar a Ghunna," who is on one of his

usual visits to town from the Black Isle. He is usually so much tormented with the juvenile fraternity that to-day he has decked himself with whin branches in order to keep the youngsters at a safe distance, and judging from Fearrachar's decorations, he will be a daring youth indeed who will attempt to tug his coat tails. See, they have already scented him, however, and are scampering down the street to give him a rousing reception. That stately gentleman in the carriage passing us, whose face and figure strongly reminds us of the Iron Duke, is Henry Baillie of Redcastle, M.P. for Inverness-shire. Hurry up! there is the steamer 'Duchess of Sutherland" coming into the Thornbush. She is now moored, and the passengers are stepping ashore after their thirty-six hours' voyage from Granton. There are other places and persons of interest in the locality, but we will deal with them on another occasion.

NOTE.—In order to give some idea of the ubiquity of the Merkinch sailor in those days, we may mention that Norman Macleod, the skipper of the "Atalanta," related in our hearing that he had six brothers who were seafaring men and had sailed on every sea, the eldest brother being master of a merchant barque. The story goes that one day while in the tropics he was pacing the quarter-deck when his eye rested on the cabin-boy, who was doing some odd jobs about the deck. He thus accosted him, "Where do you come from, my lad?" "Inverness, sir," was the reply. "The Merkinch?" "Yes, sir." "What's your father's name?" "Norman Macleod, sir." "Have you two brothers, Rory and Donald?" "Yes, sir." "Ay, my little man," said the weather-beaten, sun-browned son of Neptune, "you're my own brother." The meeting can be better

D

imagined than described. The sobriety of the Merkinch sailor of these days was remarkable, considering the fact that there were then so many public-houses in the district, and that whisky was sold at 3d. per gill. Like Jack ashore everywhere, they were of course always happy and gay when they arrived in port.

CHAPTER IX.

CAPEL INCH—THORNBUSH—THE WINDMILL.

WE will now adjourn to Rory Hovack's pie shop in Grant Street. See, there is the genial old man standing behind the counter ever ready to give his customers a hearty welcome. Let us take a seat at one of his tables and partake of some of the tit-bits of his culinary art. The place, as you observe, is not so busy as it might be, the reason being that it is summer time. Winter is Rory's harvest time, when a great business is done by him in hot pies, having in addition to his shop trade quite a small army of message lads supplying the district with the savoury viands. When the pie season is at its height the boys perambulate the streets with their pies wrapped in a clean cloth, carried in a square box which is fastened by a strap passing round the neck, the box being in front of the vendor, a small bell being attached to the side, which rings as the boys move along, so that the denizens of the neighbourhood are soon made aware when the product of Rory's oven is obtainable at their doors. You may smile, but apart from shipping and spiritualism, it may be said that the pie business is one of the most flourishing present-day industries in the Merkinch. As there is to be a great temperance meeting on the Capel Inch this evening, we will now, that we have partaken of the good things of Rory's establishment, wend our way thither. Let us turn down by way of Nelson Street. You will observe that several of the housewives are discussing the forthcoming meet-

ing at the doorways, while some are making their way
in the direction of the meeting place.   The Capel Inch
is, as you will observe, not by any means an ideal place
of recreation, it being somewhat rough and uneven and
intersected with deep ruts.   Some future Town-Council
may, in their wisdom, see fit to improve it, and make it a
fit place for outdoor sports, and a playground for the
younger people.   To the right there is Mr. Munro's shipbuilding yard, where you will observe another keel has
been laid.   The sound of the hammer, the chisel, and
the adze has now ceased for the day, it being after
working hours.   See, there are some of the workmen
who have already had supper and are daundering down
to hear what the temperance advocates have to say.
There is the platform being brought along from one of
the neighbouring houses in the shape of a strong, old-
fashioned kitchen table.   Owing to the well-directed
efforts of the speaker of the evening, the Rev. Robert
Gray Mason, the temperance cause is at present in a
flourishing state in the Highland Capital, and the
revenue of the local publicans has consequently been
reduced.   The speaker has now taken his position on
the table, and around him you will observe several well-
known townsmen, prominent among whom is Mr.
William Hutcheson of the "Journal" Office, who acts as
secretary of the Temperance Society, while by his side
is his esteemed colleague, Mr. John Macrae, watchmaker.   Behind them stands Mr. Martin, sexton, Mr.
John Melven, millwright, and right in front of the
speaker is Mr. Evan Grant and Mr. Alexander Fraser.
The audience is, as you will observe, an exceedingly large
one, the crowd, in addition to their enthusiasm in the
cause, being attracted by the personality of the lecturer,
than whom there are few more popular men in Scotland.
Listen to these burning words of his, uttered as they are

with voice and gesture which suggests to one the picture
of Paul addressing the Athenians on Mars Hill. Listen,
I say—

"It was the other day demonstrated to the satisfaction
of a large and influential meeting of merchants, ship
owners, and underwriters in the commercial capital of this
country that ships sailing on the total abstinence system
may be insured for half the premium required to cover
a risk of ships sailing on the drinking system. This is
a fact worth a world of speculation on the subject. It
has also been ascertained that men in every climate,
from the Poles to the Equator, stand climatic ravages
better without the aid of spirits than with it. And, accordingly, we find those in authority in the Army and
Navy bear testimony to the favour of this system, and
pass the highest eulogium upon it. It is, however,
ministers of the Gospel that ought to consider it, and it
concerns them chiefly to ascertain the religious bearings
of the system. Opponents charge them with making
total abstinence their religion; it is alleged that they
make a righteousness of total abstinence, and they are
charged with inculcating that taking the pledge of total
abstinence is equivalent to a change of nature. But be
it remembered it is only their opponents who charge
them with these opinions. Such doctrines are never
promulgated in the accredited organs of teetotalers, nor
are they ever avowed by teetotalers themselves. The
great object of teetotalism is to banish drunkenness, and
in its stead to substitute temperance."

That gentleman who now rises and addresses the meeting in the language of Eden is Mr. Fraser, a well-known
local temperance orator. As you are unacquainted with
the language of the speaker, I may mention that he is
just at this moment picturing a recent catastrophe in
which a number of sailors aboard ship partook too freely

of alcohol while at sea ; a storm broke over their
vessel, and so intoxicated were they that they were unable to manage the ship, which with its living freight
was dashed against the rocks—

> "Which gored its side
> Like the horns of an angry bull."

See, a number of workmen now step forward to take the
pledge in response to Mr. Mason's exhortation, while
the meeting is now dispersing.   Let us now step down
towards the Thornbush.   To the left there are a number
of young Merkinch lads engaged in quoit throwing.
Close to the quay here are the stores of Mr. Thomas
Ross ("Tommy Tar"), where a varied assortment of shipping material is kept.   Lying alongside the "Duchess of
Sutherland" there are several trading smacks, which
have just arrived, and are discharging cargo.   That
gentleman whom we see superintending affairs on the
quay is Mr. Macleod, carting contractor, upon whom de-
volves the onerous duty of seeing that the goods are
properly delivered.   I may mention that at this point six-
teen men of the 42nd Highlanders (who were on duty in
Inverness) embarked for Belgium to join their regiment
in May 1815, just a month before the Battle of Waterloo.   Among those who were present when they waved
good-bye as they sailed down the river was the late Mr.
John Rose of Kirkton.   On the opposite bank of the
river there you will observe a rude cairn which is surmounted by a heavy wooden post, and which is popularly
known as "Cairnark."   It was placed there as a guide
to mariners to keep the centre of the channel.   Considerable difficulty is experienced at this point by
mariners in consequence of there being no breakwater,
a state of matters which will doubtless be rectified in
course of time.   Here you will observe the scenery is
delightful, the landscape and seascape being beautifully

intermingled, while over all there is the glory of the setting sun. Fort-George in the distance, Ord Hill to the left, and away yonder to the right "gory Culloden" and the Nairnshire Hills, reminding one strongly of the beauties of the Welsh Coast. We have now reached the Windmill, owned by Mr. Stewart, but we will delay an inspection of this most interesting edifice until a future visit.

NOTE.—I may state that the Rev. Robert Gray Mason, although not a licentiate, was designated "the rev." by the public on account of his zeal and fervency in the cause of Gospel temperance. In 1837 he instituted the first temperance society in Inverness, the meeting place being the Chapel of Ease (Free East Church). I have in my possession his travelling map of Scotland, which shows that in the course of his mission he visited no less than 572 towns and villages, much of the distance being covered on foot. He lived well into the fifties, and was highly honoured and respected throughout the country as the pioneer missionary of temperance in Scotland. With regard to my reference to "Cairnark," I may state that one of the Lords of the Isles, at the beginning of the fourteenth century during one of his predatory expeditions, crossed over from the Black Isle and halted at this point. He immediately sent an "embassy" to the worthy Provost, demanding surrender of the town. The chief magistrate, wishing delay, sent a large supply of whisky, stating at the same time that he would receive a reply later in the evening. By sundown, however, the Islesmen, having imbibed rather freely, were under the influence of Bold John Barleycorn, and became an easy prey to the wily burghers. They were routed with much slaughter.

CHAPTER X.

WINDMILL (*continued*)—KESSOCK FERRY.

WE will now return in the direction of the Windmill, beyond the Thornbush. See yonder, coming up the Firth in full sail, is the trim schooner "Inverness-shire," just arriving from Shields with a cargo of coals for Mr. Sharp, who does an extensive business in "black diamonds" in our midst, and whose premises are in the Merkinch. A fresh breeze having sprung up, the Windmill is in full operation, and as we look at it we are reminded of a rural scene in the Netherlands. That gentleman just coming along from his residence is Mr. Stewart, the business-like and energetic proprietor. Let us have a skip through the premises, which are of a most unique character. Yonder is the kiln, which, you will observe, is at present loaded with wheat preparatory to its being ground. Let us now visit the mill proper. What a deafening sound! See out there in the yard is a jovial, light-hearted farm servant, seated on his cart awaiting his turn to get his load off, and amusing himself by singing, in not too tuneful a tone, an old-time ballad, while at the same time imitating the clatter of the mill. Listen! these are the words—

> " I am a miller to my trade,
>   And that right well you know,
> And many's a boll of meal I made
>   Since ever the mill did go."

That crowd of boys and girls you see standing around
the store are the children of working people in town,
and they are here for the purpose of receiving small
supplies of flour, which is given to them 2d. per
stone cheaper than in any of the meal stores in town.
Wages being low and trade not by any means brisk,
it is absolutely necessary that the working-class should
exercise the most rigid economy in their household
affairs, and you will readily understand that to those
with large families 2d. per stone on meal or flour means
a considerable saving. Among those barefooted chubby-
faced intelligent-looking lads awaiting their turn to
get supplied with the necessaries of life are many who
will doubtless yet make their mark in the world at
home and abroad, notwithstanding the fact that their
parents are not blessed with an over-abundance of the
good things of this earth.

We will now leave this most interesting establishment and proceed along the road in the direction of
Kessock Ferry. That genial gentleman that has just
wished us good morning is Councillor Mackenzie, the
popular lessee of the ferry, who is on his way up to
town to attend a meeting of the Council Board, of
which he is a worthy and painstaking member. Mr.
Mackenzie's zeal in attending to the comfort of passengers and the safe and speedy transit of live stock
is well known and warmly appreciated by the general
public. The country people you meet laden with
produce, such as butter, "crowdy," fowls, and eggs,
are matrons of Eilan-Dubh who have just arrived
from the other side, and are on the way up town to
barter their merchandise. The traffic on this ferry,
particularly on market days, is simply marvellous, and
it is nothing unusual to see crowded boat loads cross
and recross from daylight to dark. If on some future

occasion a railway should penetrate the north, and particularly the Black Isle, I should not be at all surprised
to see the cross-ferry traffic diminish considerably.   At
present, however, the popular lessee is reaping a good
harvest.   Look! there's Rory, Dougal, and Murdo, the
boat's crew, making a bee-line for the Kessock Inn door,
having been invited in for a dram by the cattle-
drover from Rhives.   These mariners, although they
can navigate their boat through "the seven currents,"
in mid-ferry are, I am afraid, not just quite qualified
to take a certificate at Trinity House.   They are, however, strong, hardy, reliable seamen of the good old
Highland type, and though the voyage which they
undertake about a dozen times daily is a comparatively
short one, think not that they have not sometimes
to face danger.   In tempestuous weather there are,
perhaps, few more dangerous passages than Kessock,
and it requires the steady hand and the keen eye of
the helmsman to guide the boat safely into the "jetty."
On the other side of the "jetty" there you will
observe a number of particularly strong-looking vessels.
These are the Redcastle stone-boats, and sail regularly
between the quarries there and the point.   There is
quite a trade in this stone, several of the principal
buildings in town, including the Castle, being built of
it.   We will now step along a little further and await
the arrival of the next boat from the other side while
we enjoy the scenery of the upper part of the Firth.
They are now hoisting the brown sail, and she moves
off from the jetty, while the trio who have been refreshing themselves in the Kessock Inn are making a
headlong rush down the jetty, so that they may start
from this side simultaneously with the boat on the
other side.   They have got a bit of tacking to do, you
will observe, the wind being somewhat contrary.   The

boat is now making for the jetty, so we will step along and have a look at the passengers as they disembark. You will observe the passenger list is a somewhat varied one, one of the most noticeable passengers being a blind itinerant almanac vendor, whose tall, gaunt figure is a familiar one at all the fairs throughout the north. He is just being led up the jetty by his youthful guide. What unearthly squealing is that? Oh! that's our old friend Macgitten and his flock of pigs. One has just, you will observe, accidentally slipped between the boat and the pier, and the heroic owner has un-loosed his immense red " gravat " and succeeded in casting a loop over the splattering, struggling porker, and now he has succeeded in landing him, while the others have found their way ashore, and now the entire drove slowly straggle townwards, while " Macgitten " steps into the inn to steady his nerves after the excitement of a few moments ago. It will occupy too much time to visit the classic village of Clachnaharry to-day, but as there are many interesting personages and places in and around it, we will devote part of another day to its exploration. Meantime we will retrace our steps townwards and have a chat with the genial " Macgitten," who, if he is in the humour, will doubtless give us some points on the live stock trade.

NOTE.—In the columns of *The Highland News* I observed a query lately as to the origin of the name Kessock, and I therefore take the liberty of quoting the following explanation from an authority on the subject, viz.:—" Overlooking the old burying-ground, and close beside Callander Bridge, on the north side of the Teith, the curious knoll of Tom-na-Chessaig is readily distinguished, being surmounted by a flagstaff.

The mound is circular in shape, flat on the top (where a comfortable seat has been provided by the authorities), and measures about 120 feet in circumference round the brink.   According to antiquarians it is artificial, but nothing authentic as to its origin is on record. Local tradition, however, has a word to say here, and goes the length of telling us that it was raised by water kelpies from the river in memory of Saint Kessog. This good man is said to have been an Irish prince, who left his native village of Cashel on a mission to convert the heathen inhabitants of the west.   He lived a life of great piety, and was renowned for his wisdom and learning, and Tom-na-Chessaig marks the spot where this early Christian missionary is believed to have preached to the ancient Gaels in the dim and distant past.   Those old-world missionaries improved the lot of the natives in many ways, particularly in the progress of agriculture, establishing meal mills, and instituting fairs and festivals.   At the time of the Reformation, however, the festivals were abolished, although St. Kessog's Fair is still held in Callander in the early spring.   St. Kessog's name was long a highly-cherished one all over Scotland, as shown by the fact that the church of Auchterarder knew him as their patron saint, and that the ferry between Inverness and the Black Isle is named in memory of his visit to the north." With reference to my allusion to Redcastle, it may be interesting to know that the parish of Killearnan is so called from its being the last resting-place of Earnan, a Danish prince, who invaded this country in the early part of the Christian Era.   In dealing with my allusion to the children, who in days gone by used to visit the windmill, I might mention such illustrious names as the late Hon. Alexander Fraser, a native of the Leachkin, and a prominent colonial politician, the late

General William Macbean, V.C., of whom every
Invernessian is so justly proud, the late Hugh Miller,
one of the civic authorities of the city of Toronto, Mr.
Maclean, another prominent citizen of the capital of
Ontario, and many other successful men who have
made their influence felt for good in different parts of
the globe.

CHAPTER XI.

CLACHNAHARRY—CALEDONIAN CANAL—MONUMENT—THE
WELL—MUIRTOWN HOUSE—MUIRTOWN BRIDGE.

WE are now in the ancient and classic village of
Clachnaharry.   As the day is fine and the roadways in
good condition, we will endeavour to wend our way
through the labyrinthine mazes of its principal thoroughfares.   The architecture of the public and residential
buildings are, as you will observe, of a most primitive
character.   Do not these little white-washed thatched
cottages call to your remembrance that fine old Scotch
song, "The Auld Hoose"?—

> "O! the auld hoose, the auld hoose,
>   What tho' the rooms were wee,
> Kind hearts were dwelling there,
>   And bairnies fu' o' glee."

I doubt not that on many a foreign strand stalwart
Clachnaharrians have time and again sung these lines,
having in their mind's eye as they did so one or other
of those lowly thatched cottages which they called
home, and you know that to the Scotchman home—that
is, the home of the childhood—is the only spot on earth,
and he also says, though the song be not Scotch—

> "Where'er I may wander or ever I may roam,
>   Be it ever so humble there's no place like home."

We are presently on the King's highway leading to
the northern counties.   That low-roofed, comfortable
dwelling to our right is, I need hardly say, the most
important edifice in the village, for, as you will observe

from the sign, it is the Clachnaharry Inn, which is tenanted by Mr. Mackintosh, an ideal host, who, along with his better half, is always attentive to his customers. He is highly esteemed by the villagers. The worthy couple have around them a rising family of lads and lassies, who we have no doubt will yet rise to fill useful positions in society. That fine portly-looking gentleman with an intellectual and studious cast of countenance, who is just coming towards us from the direction of his trim and well-kept villa, is Mr. George May, the chief engineer of the Caledonion Canal. He is evidently expecting the mail coach, which is just due. By his side is his faithful and attentive man-servant, Tom Fraser, who was one of the workmen who took part in the construction of the Canal, and who has been more or less connected with it ever since. Listen! there is Angus Mackay, the guard of the mail coach "Wellington," blowing his merry horn, and now you can hear the rattle of the wheels as the coach comes up the brae. See, there it is, and you will observe it has a fair load of outside passengers. Ah! there is the gentleman Mr. May is looking for seated inside the coach engrossed in the leading article of the *Scotsman*. His name is Vansittart, and he is one of the few Commissioners of the Canal, who is on his way from London to his Caithness residence. Ah! he has now caught sight of Mr. May, and you will observe their greeting is most cordial. Their interview will be but brief, but, as they are both thorough business gentlemen, the time at their disposal will doubtless suffice them to transact their business. That is the starting signal that Angus has just blown, and see the "wheelers" and the "leaders" are again on the road, and in a few moments will be lost to view round the curve as they speed on their northern journey. Let us now stroll down to Mr. Hossack's boat-

building yard. Being comparative strangers in the
village, we are attracting considerable attention, you will
observe. Can't you see the housewives all standing in
the doorways, while the children have ceased from their
games and are gazing at us open-mouthed, clearly showing that the visits of strangers to the interior of the
village are like those of the angels, few and far between.
The hens are scrambling away with alarming cackle,
while the very dogs appear to be disputing our right to
invade "the city." We have now reached the boat-building yard. Things seem to be pretty busy for I observe
Mr. Hossack has no less than three boats under course
of construction. Further along Mr. Fraser ("Byron") is
also busily engaged in boat-building. They are evidently
making preparations for the coming fishing season, as
some of the old boats are getting the worse of the wear
and tear of wind and tide. Over at the Sea Lock there
is the tugboat "Samson," with a barque laden with
guano from Callao in tow, while out in the Firth beyond
are several of the village boats engaged in line fishing.
We will now pass westward through the village and
visit the Priesag Well, from which the villagers receive
their water supply. See, there are several matrons and
damsels coming towards us with their hoops and pails,
and, judging from their merriment, they are evidently
having some joke at our expense. What was that that
prim-looking, fair-haired maiden said about "Invernessians" as we passed? It doesn't matter much anyway. We are now at the well, and let us partake of a
draught of this "water pure from the sparkling rill,"
which can safely be said never left any man in the ditch.
This, then, is the spot where the village gossip is retailed,
and I have no doubt that the guid wife on many occasions,
while hauling her next door neighbour over the coals at
this point and also along the road, often forgets that the

goodman is in from work and waiting for his supper with a scowl on his countenance. To our right there is an historic spot where a clan battle was fought away back in these times, when it was—

> " The good old rule, the simple plan,
> They may take who have the power,
> And they may keep who can."

We will now retrace our steps in the direction of the Canal. Let us have a look in at " the smiddy." That hardy son of Vulcan you see at the anvil is James Thom, the Canal blacksmith. His son William, who has just returned from town, is blowing the bellows. They have ceased from their labours for a moment, and hark! the old man seems to be warning William in connection with some serious matter. Listen; what is that he says about " the wiles of a dark-eyed maiden "? Ah! I see what the old man is at now. The maiden is a Clach-naharry beauty, and the young man is enamoured of her. We will now get down on to the high road and return by way of Muirtown. That coach which has just passed us is that of Mr. Fraser of Lovat. He is accompanied by his eldest son Simon, who has just returned from school for a short vacation. Here are three gigs coming along, the first being occupied by Mr. John Rose, Kirkton; the next by Mr. John Fraser, Inchberry; and Mr. Colin Chisholm, Phopachy, three well-known local agriculturists, who are just returning from town where they have been attending market. To the left is the tollhouse, at which considerable business is done in the way of tollage, although, as is the case at all other tolls, there are many attempts made (sometimes successful, but at all times hazardous) to evade dues. A few yards to the right there is the once famous curative well, which Mr. Duff of Muirtown has recently enclosed and dedi-cated the well to " Lucy, the Nymph of the Fountain."

E

We are now at the entrance to Muirtown House, the
residence of Mr. Huntly R. Duff. The two beautifully-
modelled metal lions surmounting the pillars are presumably the supporters of the arms of the Duff family.
We are now in the vicinity of Muirtown Bridge, where
we meet old Donald Treasurer, a well-known Muirtown
Green worthy, bearing his favourite son of his old age,
" Jot," on his back, in addition to a weight of years. He is
an eccentric old chap. Let us ask him where he is bound
for. What was that he said in reply to my question?
" A'm going to the Cape to see Jimmy, and A'm following the sun," wasn't that what he said? Just such an
answer as might be expected from Donald. His knowledge of geography is apparently somewhat vague, or, if
not, his sense of humour does not run in the ordinary
channels. He has a son at the Cape, and it is just possible
that he imagines he can reach him by travelling in the
direction of the North Cape. Let us hope that ere the
sun sinks in the west Donald and his charge will be safely
esconced by his cosy ingle-neuk in Davis Square. We
will now cross the Canal by the Muirtown swing-bridge.
That building to the left is the Muirtown Hotel; while
those men you see standing by the wharf looking
anxiously down in the direction of Clachnaharry are a
squad of quay labourers watching the guano ship
entering the Muirtown Basin. They have already been
hired to discharge her, and are speculating how much
apiece they will be able to knock out of the job. As
time is limited, we will now hurry into town, and on a
future occasion again return to this locality.

Note.—The word " Clachnaharry " is usually taken
to mean " The Watchman's Stone," where it was generally supposed the authorities of Inverness in the olden
time used to place a sentinal to guard against incursions

of marauding clansmen, but on the authority of Mr. Whyte Cullaird, an eminent Gaelic scholar, the word is said to signify "Clach-na-h-eithre," or "The Stone of the Boat," where in ancient times the natives used to land their small boats from the opposite side of the Firth in consequence of not being able to navigate the "seven tides" at Kessock. The Preesag Well, which has from time immemorial been the source of water supply for the village, lies to the west alongside the high road, while on a rocky eminence overlooking the village is a monument erected by the late H. R. Duff of Muirtown. It consists of a column fourteen feet high, encircled by an iron railing. The column is surmounted by a winged Mercury. On the sides of the monument are inscribed the words, "Munro and Clan Chattan." There are several accounts of the battle, which was fought in the fifteenth century, but the only authentic one is that of Mackintosh, Kinrara, which will be found in the works of Dr. Fraser Mackintosh. Near the toll-house, between Clachnaharry and Muirtown, there is a pathway leading to a well a few yards off the high road. It is said that the Marquis of Montrose, while on his way from Assynt to Edinburgh as a prisoner in 1650, enjoyed a draught of its cooling waters. It was said to possess curative properties, but in consequence of a soldier's wife having washed her fever-stricken babe in it, the virtue ceased. It may be interesting to know that Mr. Thomas Fraser, who is referred to above, died recently in Elgin at the patriarchal age of 104 years. The circumstances which gave place to the fight, which the monument on the rocks above Clachnaharry commemorates, have been frequently narrated, but seldom correctly, and it is but little known that the principal bctors were not only reconciled, but subsequently aecame brothers-in-law, Malcolm Oig, afterwards referred to, marrying Janet Munro, a sister of his opponent in the struggle. Dr. Fraser Mackintosh is of opinion that the following account of the circumstances which led to the engagement, given by Mackintosh of Kinrara, is the most reliable:—" In 1454 a sudden and un-expected conflict sprung up between Malcolm Mac-intosh, commonly called Gillicallum Oig Mac Mic-Gillicullum Bey, grandson of the aforesaid Malcolm Mackintosh (of Mackintosh), and John Munro, tutor of Fowlis, a very keen contention followed. The origin of it was this : John Munro was second son of Hugh Munro of Fowlis, and acted as tutor to John Munro, his nephew, by his brother George Munro of Fowlis. Returning from a tour to the South for despatching his pupil's business, a dissension took place between him and the inhabitants of Strathardle. He was contemptu-ously treated, and loaded with great abuse. Intent upon revenge, he comes home informing his friends and relations of the insult he has sustained, and implores their assistance. At the head of two hundred chosen men he advances with all possible speed, and before his approach is observed, enters Strathardle, ravages the country, and carries off the herds of cattle. At the River Findhorn, on his return, the aforesaid Malcolm Oig meets him by accident, and, understanding the matter, is urged by the young men that follow him to demand a part of the plunder. John offers him twenty-four cows and a bull, which Malcolm Oig proudly and rashly rejects, insisting on no less than one-third part. John treats his demand with scorn, and proceeds on his way, determined to give none. Malcolm Oig incensed, instantly com-municates this to his friends, and immediately commands the inhabitants of Petty and Lochardhill to follow John and obstruct his progress, until he with the men of Strathnairn shall have come up. His commands are obeyed. They pursue John beyond the water of Ness, and overtake him at a lake called Clachnaharry. He (John) sends off forty men with the booty and encourages the rest to fight. A fierce conflict ensues, a few fall on each side. John, almost slain, is left among the dead, but Lord Lovat, upon better information, takes care of his recovery, John, afterwards called Baichlich, *i.e.*, Maimed, because he lost his hand in the engagement. From him descended the family of Milltown. Malcolm Oig was not present at the battle, which arose from his temerity, for the conflict took place before he came up."

CHAPTER XII.

As our time was limited during our recent visit to
Muirtown, we were unable to visit the stately mansion-
house of Major H. R. Duff, and we will accordingly do
so to-day. Let us pass through the Lions' Gate.
Observe how docile and domesticated the animals look.
How often have the youthful fraternity gazed open-
mouthed at them, watching to see them change places,
for it is said that they do so every time they HEAR the
clock strike one.   Youthful credulity goes a great length,
but I have even seen pretty old-fashioned children
gulled with the same story, it never once occurring to
them that the " lions " of course cannot possibly hear
the clock strike. We will now proceed along the
beautiful avenue, as a certain part of the grounds are
open to the public.   Yonder handsome elderly gentleman and stately-looking lady walking arm-in-arm along
the side path are Major and Mrs. Duff. The name
Duff has been more or less associated with the history
of Inverness for several centuries, several of the family
having occupied the civic chair of our royal burgh.
The mansion-house, which was rebuilt some years ago,
is designed on Italian architectural lines. The house
was the scene of many events, grave and gay, in the
history of the family.   We will now return to the high
road.   That is Mr. Forbes, the civil and obliging toll-
keeper, whom you see passing the gateway. He is on

his way into town, as is his usual custom. Although the average toll-keeper is generally at loggerheads with the public, who protest against tollage, Mr. Forbes by his affability is quite a favourite, and the dues are, as a rule, paid with seeming cheerfulness to him. That bog on the opposite side of the road, which was for a long time an eyesore, is now being rapidly filled up by ballast brought over from the Emerald Isle by ships which come into Muirtown Wharf for potatoes. I shouldn't be at all surprised if the " dear little shamrock " is to be found growing there. If we had time to look we might find it. Irishmen tell us that the shamrock will only grow on Irish soil. Well, then, there it is in shiploads. That medium-sized gentleman whom you see on the Canal bank following the vocation of Izaak Walton is Mr. Archibald Tait, perfumer, whose shop is on Church Street near the Caledonian Hotel, while that elderly man by his side is Jeems Macdougall, who is in his employment. Jeems is a fly-hook dresser by profession, and is supposed to be one of the most experienced anglers in the North of Scotland, which earned for him the sobriquet of the "Northern Switcher." Mr. Tait does not seem to have much luck to-day, and methinks he might well say in very much the style of Tom Hood—

> " For trout I've learned how to try
> By a method of Walton's own showing,
> But I very much doubt
> I will catch little trout
> In a path that's devoted to towing."

We will now return again to Muirtown Bridge, and take a stroll down along the wharf. That white building at the water edge and close by the crane is the dwelling-house of Mr. Hugh Fraser, lock-keeper, and his two boys, Robert and George, who are standing in the doorway looking down in the direction of the entrance where Mr. Fraser is engaged in letting in the potato schooner " Albatross." To the back of the lock-keeper's house is Mr. James Sutherland's Glenalbyn Distillery. The liquor distilled here is supposed to possess rare qualities, and is much in demand all over the country. That barque moored close by is the " Southern Cross," which we observed coming up the Canal during our last visit. Her cargo of guano has, you will observe, been discharged, and the crew are busily getting underway for the outward voyage. We will now retrace our steps in the direction of the bridge. There is Mr. Sutherland, the genial host of the Muir-town Hotel, standing at the door in the act of receiving visitors, whom we have no doubt he will treat with Highland hospitality. Of course you understand that he is also the owner of the distillery. He is a thorough business man and a member of the Town-Council, and may yet be called upon to occupy the civic chair. He also takes quite an interest in church matters, and is one of the leading members of the High Church. Right opposite the Muirtown Hotel is the shop of Mr. Harold, provision merchant. The establishment, as you will observe, is not of a very pretentious character, but it is a well-known fact that a fair amount of business is done from one end of the year to the other, as is natu-rally to be expected from the large shipping trade at this point. Mr. Harold is much respected by all with whom he has dealings, and it is a fact worthy of note that he is as civil and affable to the very poorest of his customers as he is to those who are in more affluent circumstances. I shall never forget standing at his counter one day while he was conversing to a lady of the better class. A poor but decently clad woman came in, and laying a small jug on the counter, asked for "a pennyworth of treacle." He spoke to her as affably and attended to her order as cheerfully as if it had been one upon which he would have reaped a large profit. When the poor woman left, the haughty dame, who had to stand aside while he was measuring out the treacle, remarked, "It's a wonder you would be bothered with trifling orders like that, Mr. Harold." He looked at her for a moment and said, "She paid ready money, you observed, and that's more than the most of my customers do." I need hardly say that she said no more, for the probability was that she owed Mr. Harold a heavy bill for groceries. See, there he is accompanying the captain of the "Southern Cross" to the door. The mariner has lately been giving him an order for provisions. That building which you see a little distance from Mr. Harold's shop is the Ropework, but we may probably be able to visit it on another occasion. The ground for some distance around it is locally known as Poll a' Criadh (the Clay Hole). Listen! there is the whistle of Messrs. David Hutchison & Co.'s steamer "The Edinburgh Castle," as she is nearing the Tomnahurich Bridge. Let us stroll leisurely up to the top lock and see her arriving. See, there she is now coming round the bend, and you will observe that the deck is crowded with a goodly number of passengers. That smart, pleasant-looking gentleman standing on the paddle-box is Captain Peter Turner, who is a general favourite among all classes. It does not take his deck hands and himself long to moor the vessel. All is bustle now among the passengers, who are anxious about their luggage. The captain is now bidding good-bye to several ladies and gentlemen who have been passengers, and to whom all along the route he had been pointing out the many unrivalled beauties of lake, mountain, and stream. The worthy captain is

not only known for his amiability but also as a meteoro-
logist, his weather forecasts being generally very
accurate.   Mr. Carruthers of the *Courier* once said,
" How very pleasant it would be to enjoy a sail down
the Canal sitting alongside of Scott and Burns, and
listening to their conversation on the varied beauties of
the scenes ! "   We would venture to prefer Scott along
with the travel-loving Byron.   We will now cross the
top lock and look at what is now known as the
" Double Dykes," which is all that remains of General
Wade's road crossing by the west of Craig Phadrick to
Beauly and the north.   The double dykes is the
favourite haunt of our popular song bird, the rose
linnet.   By-the-by, I had almost forgotten to relate to
you the particulars of the formation of the Canal.   The
construction of a waterway between the east and west
coast was a scheme which had long been in contempla-
tion, and Mrs. Grant of Laggan, in her " Letters from
the Mountains," under date 1775, observed the desira-
bility of such a canal, and indeed, if I remember correctly, about that time it was surveyed by James Watt.
After consideration the Government decided in 1803 to
go on with the work.   A writer about that time stated
that it would be the greatest work of modern times,
and would cost £300,000 and yield a revenue of £40,000
per annum, and that ships passing through the Canal
with cargoes of flax for Dundee would thus avoid the
rather dangerous passage of the Pentland Firth.   The
Government of the day entrusted the engineering work
to Thomas Telford, the celebrated engineer.   Hundreds
of men were occupied in the construction of it for the
long period of twenty years, and it was not completed
until 1823.   The Canal is, I understand, 61½ miles long,
37½ miles being through the different lochs and 23½ miles
by cuts.   There are twenty-eight locks.   Altogether it has

been a huge undertaking, and I may just mention that it was in the autumn of 1823 it was opened, when the little steamer "Stirling Castle" left Muirtown on its first voyage to the western sea. The vessel was gaily decorated with bunting, and aboard were the Canal Commissioners and several privileged parties, while there was also a band of pipers present. Altogether it was one of the most notable events in the history of the period, and might well be termed the advent of a new method of travelling in the Highlands. It is now about to be closed for repairs, and in some parts reconstruction, and will in all likelihood be closed for some years. The work is entrusted to Mr. George May, under whose tactful and skilful management we have not the slightest doubt it will be carried out to the entire satisfaction of the Commissioners. I may here remark that, although the Canal has and will continue to be a valuable asset in the commerce of the country, it has never rendered that return which its projectors anticipated. The Italians say,

SEE NAPLES AND DIE,

but to you who never did so, I would re-echo the sentiment and say, "Pass through the Caledonian Canal, see the Great Glen, and don't die." The day is now far advanced, and we had better return to town. I will describe to you Telford Street and some of the places in its vicinity during our next walk.

NOTE.—It will doubtless be interesting to know that Mr. Thomas Telford, whose portrait was recently presented to the Inverness Town-Council, was a native of Dumfriesshire, and was a relative of the late esteemed ex-Bailie Elliot. It may not be generally known to football enthusiasts that the Poll à Chriadh is the old-time name of the Caledonian Football Ground. The recent keen competition evinced between the trans- atlantic steam companies reminds me of a similar fracas which took place between rival companies sailing on the Canal some time after the Canal was open for passenger traffic. At the time referred to the one company brought the fare to Glasgow down to sixpence, the rival company brought the fare down to nothing and a bottle of porter thrown in; but, of course, this soon worked its own cure. The Caledonian Canal passage was for many years the favourite route for the people of Inverness travelling to and from the second city of the Empire.

CHAPTER XIII.

THE MUIRTOWN ROPEWORK—TELFORD—MUIRTOWN NURSERIES—TELFORD ROAD—ABBAN STREET.

As you will remember, I promised on our last visit to the Muirtown district to describe to you another of the Inverness industries, viz., the Muirtown Ropework, which employs a considerable number of men and boys. There, standing at the office door giving some instruction to his foreman, is the much-respected proprietor, Mr. Chisholm, who takes a great interest in his employees, many of whom reside at the Big Green. Mr. Chisholm has, along with Mr. Alexander Macdonald, a partnership in the Tanworks in Gilbert Street. Mr. Chisholm is a prominent member of the Catholic communion, and is looked up to as an excellent business gentleman. We will now stroll along Telford Street, which is named after Thomas Telford, the celebrated engineer, who, as I already told you, carried out the construction of the Caledonian Canal. This scheme, however, great as it was, was only but a small part of the great man's work. A few facts regarding him, which I omitted to mention during our last stroll, may interest you. Like not a few other Scotch geniuses who have made and are likely to make their mark, notably Hugh Miller, who is climbing the ladder of fame, Telford began life as a stonemason, and, strange to say, amid his toils he even attempted, and not unsuccessfully, to ascend the steeps of sunlit Parnassus, for he dabbled in verse of more than ordinary merit in the homely doric of his native Scottish vale. Later on, in graphic language, he wrote his own autobiography, besides writing other excellent treatises on various subjects. It was, however, in the more practical field of engineering that he made his mark, not only at home but on the Continent. He was indeed a most wonderful man, his versatility being truly marvellous. It was he who designed the magnificent bridge across the Tweed at Kelso, the Broomielaw at Glasgow, the Dean Bridge at Edinburgh—in fact he designed during the course of his distinguished career over 1200 bridges in different parts of the kingdom, while as a roadmaker he executed more than 1000 miles in the Highlands, Lanarkshire, and Dumfriesshire. The construction of the Ellesmere Canal he also planned and superintended, while in 1808 and 1813 he was invited to go to Sweden to report on the projected scheme for connecting Lake Wener with the Baltic, while he also superintended the works in connection with the Gotha Canal by which this was effected, for which he was highly honoured by the Swedish Government. He was also consulted by the home and Russian Governments on various great schemes. His useful life came to a close, and his last survey was completed some ten years ago (1834), when he passed over to the " Great Beyond." It may safely be said that few men have left behind on this mundane sphere more magnificent monuments and undying memorials to their skill and genius than Thomas Telford, the Dumfriesshire shepherd's son, who first saw light 'mid the rural scenes of lovely Eskdale. Even the very road upon which we now stand was constructed under his superintendence, and, as you will observe, it is well adapted for all kinds of traffic, and is most unlike many of the narrow thoroughfares in the vicinity. On the left there is the beautiful town mansion of Mr. Mason, Gorthlick. It is, as you will see, built of the beautiful redstone from Redcastle Quarries. Mr. Mason is an advanced agriculturist, and is doing a great work as a land improver, his farm of Gorthlick being indeed a model one. There he is standing at the gate conversing with our esteemed Sheriff-Substitute, William Hansom Colquhoun, and Mr. Alexander Mactavish, Town-Clerk, who are on their way, as is their custom, to dine with Major Duff, the genial and hospitable laird of Muirtown. The Sheriff, as you will notice, well merits the appellation "Handsome," his tall dignified figure, refined, intellectual countenance, and gentlemanly bearing being much commented on and admired by the populace. Hark! they are discussing some political question. Ay, just as I thought, they are on the Irish question, and are discussing the sudden arrest of Dan O'Connell and his colleagues. The party has just been joined by Mr. James Gordon ("Jamie Eyeglass"), corn merchant, who has just, along with Mr. Mason, concluded the purchase of an extensive tract of growing timber at Blackwood, Leys. I do not think that those gentlemen will be like the timber merchant who used to say "that he never bought a forest but that he bought the forester also." On the opposite side of the road are the Muirtown Nurseries, comprising about twenty acres, which are rented by Howden Brothers, who represent the firm of Messrs. Lawson & Son, George IV. Bridge, Edinburgh. There has recently been a great revival in the work of arboriculture throughout the north, and this firm is doing an excellent business. Quite a large number of men and women are, as you will observe, employed in the weeding process. They are mostly residents of Muirtown Green. Their occupation, as you will observe, is of a most laborious nature. The continual stooping is very

much more trying than if they were engaged in more
arduous manual labour.   Just inside the gate there is
Mr. Alexander Macphail, an employee of the firm, who
has taken a run over from their warehouse on High
Street.   He is looking after some shrubs and plants
which have been ordered.   Mr. Macphail is a well-
known citizen, and has recently been elected an
elder of the West Parish Church.   There is every prospect of further development of the nursery and of this
most beneficial industry in the future.   We are now at
the head of Telford Road.   The stately buildings to our
left, also of Redcastle stone, were erected in 1810,
and are evidently part of the material which was left
over in connection with the building of the stone work
at the Canal.   They are the residences of business
men in town.   Just entering the door of his house
there is the smart figure of one of Inverness' best-
known and ablest citizens, Mr. Alexander Dallas,
solicitor.   Listen! he is cracking a joke in his own in-
imitable way with that Nairn fishwife, who has just
been disposing of the finny denizens of the deep to his
household.   He is, by-the-by, a native of the Nairn
district—Geddes, if I remember correctly.   Mr. Dallas
is a great humorist, and is well known as an anti-
quarian, there being few better qualified to write a
history of Inverness.   He is also an exceptionally
clever lawyer, and, indeed, few of his fellows can
"tackle" him in debate.   We will now turn down
Telford Road.   It seems to me a pity that the names
of these two thoroughfares should be synonymous, as to
strangers the fact of the one being called Telford Street
and the other Telford Road is somewhat confusing.
The latter might have appropriately been called
Victoria Road in honour of our young Queen.   We
will now turn into that old-world locality known as the

Abbey; but we may look in vain for anything that bears any resemblance whatever to a sacred edifice, as the name indicates, although it is just possible that "the friars of orders grey" who had their residence on the opposite side of the river might have had some connection with it. If I had thought of it a few minutes ago I might have asked Mr. Dallas for some information as to the origin of the name, as he is, as I have already stated, an authority on such matters. There are various theories as to why this district bears an ecclesiastical name, but I am afraid they are all apocryphal. However, we will let the matter drop, and may yet be able to ascertain something authentic on the subject. Right in front of us there is a small pond, which rises and falls the height of the river according to the tide. This is said to have been the ancient bed of the river, and is locally known as the Abbey Loch. It is much resorted to in the winter time by the youthful fraternity as a sliding pond. We are now at the few cottages in the locality with their lancet windows. One of the cottagers, Rory Mackenzie, the shoemaker, has just come to his doorway for his afternoon smoke. In early life Rory had an excellent business in town, and could at one time append to his name that dignified and exalted title, "Burgess of Inverness," and was wont to sit in the Trades' Loft in the Gaelic Church gallery in all the glory of brown coat, embroidered waistcoat, knee-breeches, silk stockings, shoes, and buckles. Times have changed, however, with this old son of St. Crispin, and luck has, unhappily, gone against him; and to-day, in place of this semi-regal garb, he is decked with his old leathern apron. In his day he has had many luxuries, but to-day all he can afford to soothe himself with is, as he says himself, "a smoke of the pipe." That is his neighbour, Angus Mackay

F

("Angy Threadie"), the tailor, who has joined him, and as they are both remarkably intelligent men, their conversation is, I doubt not, of an edifying and elevating nature. Both are lonely men—old bachelors. If I could dare anticipate, however, I might venture to say that they will yet take unto themselves wives. The locality is at present quite rural in its aspect, but as the years go by and the burgh extends its borders, it will, I have no doubt, be largely taken advantage of for building purposes. Having now explored the Abbey, we will emerge into Huntly Street, which, along with Gilbert Street, I will describe to you during our next stroll together.

NOTE.—I may mention that it was not for some years after the date of which I write that the Telford Street Militia Barracks were erected—1856.

CHAPTER XIV.

HUNTLY STREET—HUNTLY PLACE—VETERAN ROW—
TANNERY.

HAVING explored the locality known as "Sraid nah-Abhann"—"the Street of the River," as the older people call it—we will this evening take a stroll along Huntly Street, which is so named after Major Huntly R. Duff, to whom I have already referred. These tall, three-storeyed dwelling-houses on Huntly Place, which stand out as a landmark from various points, were erected very early in the century as better-class residences. The nearest one is occupied by the Rev. James Kennedy, minister of the Congregational Church in Fraser Street. The reverend, I might almost say venerable, gentleman is a most useful and deservedly popular minister in town. He first saw the light in Inverallan in 1777, and having gone through the usual curriculum, he was appointed Congregational minister in the parish of Abernethy, and came to Inverness about the opening years of the century. The Congregational body in town then worshipped in a small building in Bank Street, which is now used as a smithy or farriery. The present church was built in 1821, and the congregation is a model one, at least from the dissenters point of view. It is composed of many well-to-do citizens, and so popular is Mr. Kennedy, that regret has often been expressed that a very much larger church was not erected, in order that the large crowds which gather to hear him Sabbath after Sabbath might be comfortably accommodated. He is an excellent preacher, his sermons being elegant in diction and profound in thought, while his delivery is most pleasing. Look, there is Mr. Kennedy slowly descending the steps of his residence, and from his appearance you will readily see that when I described him as venerable I was not exaggerating in the slightest degree. The long, rapidly whitening locks and the thoughtful, intellectual cast of countenance reminds one of the portraits of the great evangelical preacher, John Wesley. To the right there is what is known as Wells Foundry, and that group of young lads you see sitting and "skylarking" beside these newly-finished boilers in front of the establishment have evidently caught sight of Mr. Kennedy, for they have suddenly quietened down, and their language, as you can hear, has become wonderfully decorous. One of them, however, who is evidently a good deal bolder than the others, insists on smoking a clay pipe, although he is doubtless well aware that Mr. Kennedy will check him if he notices him. Ah! the pastor evidently intends to converse with them, as he is making straight across the roadway in their direction. Let us get a little closer until we hear the nature of the conversation. Hark! he has just asked the youthful smoker for "one blast" of his pipe. They all seem to be taken aback, and shyly and reluctantly the boy, now somewhat crestfallen, hands him his new clay pipe. Instead of placing it in his mouth, as the lads expected, Mr. Kennedy drops it to the ground, places his heel on it, and grinds it to powder, at the same time remarking, "Did not I ask but for 'one blast,' boys?" He now, with a smile of satisfaction, turns away, and is joined by his son, Mr. John Kennedy, who is home from the Theological Hall, while that tall, dark-complexioned young gentleman who is also approaching is the reverend gentleman's foster son, Mr. Donaldson, also a student. An eminent writer says, "We should not prophesy unless we know," but I have no hesitation in saying, from what I already know of them, that both these gentlemen will yet take a high place in their respective professions. We will now continue our course along Huntly Place. At his door stands the stalwart, military form of Lieutenant Lobban, whose stern, grim countenance indicates that he has smelt powder on many a hard-fought field, while that other military-looking gentleman coming along is Mr. James Fraser of Dochgarroch. He served with his regiment as a lieutenant in the Peninsular War, and was present at the Battle of Vimiera under Wellington in 1809, and subsequently won laurels at the Battle of Orthes. He is to me the beau-ideal of a Highland officer, his magnificent figure, splendid bearing, and resolute disposition stamping him as one born to command. It is a matter of surprise to me that he has not been able to attain to higher rank in his profession, but in those "piping times of peace" even a captain's commission would be worth a king's ransom. Lieutenant Fraser is a staunch member of the High Church, and if you have ever been in that sacred edifice you may have noticed him seated at all the diets of worship in the seat covered with green baize, close to the east door. He is altogether an admirable citizen and a most popular gentleman, and as he is yet hale and hearty, he has, it is hoped, many years of usefulness before him. We are now on Veteran Row, which has doubtless derived its name from the fact that several of the cottages on it were erected by the soldiers who had returned from the Continental wars early in the century. That medium-sized gentleman coming towards us, whose thoughtful face indicates his calling, is Mr. John Douglas, the master of the Merkinch School, under Bell's Trust, who is just returning from his navigation class, where the young lads of the locality are taught at least the theory of that useful science which will enable them in after years to sail 'neath home and alien skies. He is an excellent teacher, and has turned out many scholars who have proved a credit to themselves, their native town, and their teacher. We are now in the vicinity of "the tanyard," or Tannery, and judging from the exterior of the erection, it appears to us to have been built before the days of architecture, for it is one of the most ugly structures that ever cast its shadow on any locality. That group of men you see up to their knees in the river are the skinners, who are preparing their skins for further operations. There in the doorway is Mr. Alexander Macdonald, the senior partner of the firm (Messrs. Macdonald & Chisholm). He is just handing a letter to "Hugh," the man-of-all-work, to take to the wine office on High Street. "Hugh" is a well-known character, but in his own quiet, inoffensive way was useful. He learned very adroitly to be able to supply wind to the organ in the Catholic Chapel. Mr. Macdonald, the proprietor, is one of the Macdonalds of Glenalladale, and was for some years factor on the extensive Lovat estates. In addition to his business he has an extensive wholesale wine and spirit establishment, and is a shrewd and capable man of business, whose large-heartedness and genuine benevolence is much appreciated in the community. We are now once more at the corner of Grant Street, where the usual group of mariners are congregated. There is Skipper John Mackenzie ("Gairloch") advising his men to get in readiness to sail for Sunderland in a few days with a cargo of props. That group of men and women who have just crossed the bridge from the opposite side are a party of harvesters, as you will observe from the hooks and pitchers which they carry. They look fatigued after their hard day's work, but it is consoling for them to know (to use the words of Longfellow), that

> "Something attempted, something done,
> Has earned a night's repose."

The day is not surely far distant when the farmer, by a less laborious and speedier method, will be enabled to cut his crops. Of all wage-earners, the harvester is the most industrious and hard-working. Would you be surprised to learn that experts with the "hook" from these northern parts are in great demand among the farmers of the Lothians, and it is nothing uncommon for large numbers of men and women from the Highlands to journey on foot to the Lowlands for the purpose of taking part in the harvest, and to again return at its conclusion as light-hearted and light-footed as the proverbial "Irish ragman." As the sun is now setting behind the bens, and as we have some other business to attend to ere we retire to rest, we will not this evening continue our perambulations further. I shall next introduce you to the salmon fishers in Friars' Shott.

NOTE.—There are, I daresay, few, if any, alive now who remember the old Congregational Chapel in Bank Street, to which I have alluded above, when the structure was used as a sacred edifice. Many of the older inhabitants will, however, doubtless remember it as a smithy. If my memory serves me rightly, the blacksmith who occupied it was Mr. Duncan Macfarquhar. On the same site now stands the Highland Brigade Orderly Room. The Rev. Mr. Kennedy's son, to whom I allude above, was in after years known as the Rev. Dr. John Kennedy of Stepney, who, as an evangelical preacher, had in his day few equals; while Mr. Donaldson, his foster-brother, was none other than Professor Donaldson, one of the best scholars of Modern Athens.

CHAPTER XV.

WELLS' FOUNDRY—WELLS STREET—FRIARS' SHOTT.

As you will remember, we last parted on Veteran Row,
and this evening we again find ourselves in the same
locality.   We will, as arranged, stroll southward in the
direction of Friars' Shott and Wells Street, and as the
weather is exceptionally fine, our stroll will, I trust,
prove both pleasant and profitable.   See, many of the
residents of the Row are standing at their doorways,—
the men smoking their evening pipe, the women retailing the latest bit of gossip, and the children frolicking
about in the roadway and amusing themselves as only
children can.   That middle-aged man hurrying up
behind us with a parcel under his arm is John Fraser
("Johnnie Setterday"), the local tailor, whose residence
is at No. 5.   The contents of the parcel consist of the
cloth for a reefing jacket for one of "Gairloch's" seamen, and as he has promised it by "Setterday," on
which day the man sails, he is evidently very anxious
to get started at the job.   The cloth has, we have no
doubt, already been damped at Luckie Cameron's tavern
in Grant Street.   I have never been able to ascertain
how Johnnie was nicknamed "Setterday."   I should,
however, imagine that the reason is that, like other
tailors, his existence is made up of many lives, each one
ending with Saturday.   You know the average tailor
always promises everything for Saturday, and he strains
every nerve to execute his orders, so that it may with
a certain degree of truth be said that he begins life

anew each succeeding Monday morning. You ask who that tall, stout, good-looking fellow with the wallet slung over his shoulder, and who has just stepped out of the doorway of No. 7, is? That is Jeremiah Sinclair, who just came north a short time ago. The particular nature of the wares he is vending claims even more than passing interest. He sells a box containing a number of small pieces of wood dipped in sulphur, with the points covered with a preparation of phosphorus, which on being struck instantly ignites. Each small box costs one shilling, and as it is a very marked improvement on the old style of lighting, we may feel assured that the system only awaits more complete development, although we should like to see the commodity very much cheaper than it now is. You will notice how very much interested the housewives are in Jeremiah's pack, for scarcely has he slung it off his shoulder there at Johnnie Fraser's door, when he is surrounded by a bevy of women all anxious to purchase from him, but none of them seem willing to give the price he asks. They appear to think that this new and speedier method of lighting the fire to make the porridge in the morning is very much handier than the slow laborious way they have of "kenlin' the stickies" now. Ah! a purchase has been made. Three of the women have gone shares for a box, but it would appear as if the guidmen are to have the lion's share. Aren't these attempts of theirs to light their pipes amusing? Look at that old man whose hand is somewhat shaky. Why, he has nearly singed his whiskers in an attempt to light his old clay "cutty" with the "lucifer." We will now stroll up to Wells' Foundry, which, as you will remember, I pointed out to you on our last visit. Judging from the clang of metal and the sound of the hammer, business is at present remarkably brisk in this establishment. That is the proprietor, Mr. Wells, who, along with his son Jonathan, is standing at the office door. Although not exactly on business, we will have a stroll through the premises. There are various departments, you will observe, and altogether the establishment is conducted on the most approved lines, being composed of millwright, moulding, fitting, and finishing shops. That is Mr. Melven, the foreman millwright, who is giving directions to some of his men in connection with the construction of a threshing machine for New Tarbet. Mr. Melven, who is a native of Inverurie, is, as you will observe, a man of striking physique, while he is also possessed of marked individuality. He takes a great interest in church matters, and is one of the leading total abstainers in town. The Foundry is one of the principal industries in the district, and gives work to a large number of men and lads. It is to be hoped that the establishment may long continue in the same flourishing condition in which we now find it. Listen! there is the bell indicating that the day's labours are over, and, workmanlike, each grimy son of toil makes a dash for his jacket and the gate, among the first being Danny M'Swan, a well-known Green lad. We will now make our exit along with the workers, and find ourselves in Friars' Place in front of a row of trim cottages with neatly kept gardens. At her garden gate there stands Widow Cameron and her only son, Robert, who lately met with a severe accident, but who is now recovering. We will now turn into that wide and spacious thoroughfare, Wells Street, which is so named after the proprietor of the Foundry. A few doors up on the right-hand side stands Mr. James Kyle, who has lately been appointed emigration agent for the district, and also to the charge of the Wells Street Receiving Post-Office under the new Act.

Mr. Kyle, who is a most intelligent and business-like gentleman, will, we feel sure, conduct the duties devolving upon him to the satisfaction of his superiors. We have now reached the top of the street. Yonder is Mr. Grant, the plasterer, who is enjoying his evening pipe at his cottage door. Sergeant Grant, who is one of the old militia staff, dons his uniform (scarlet coat, black trousers, peaked cap, sash, and sword belt) once a month, and along with his old chum, Sergeant William Chisholm, goes and claims his pay at the Pay-Office on Petty Street. That gushet-house at the corner of Wells Street and Muirtown Street is the Steamboat Inn, which is indicated by a representation of a steamboat full steam ahead, yet, strange to say, is

"As idle as a painted ship upon a painted ocean."

On his doorstep is mine host, Mr. James Kennedy, good-naturedly conversing with Mr. Bisset, stoneware merchant, whose business is a little way up Muirtown Street, or, as it was formerly called, Beauly Street. We will now retrace our steps along Wells Street. Standing at the edge of the kerbstone is William Macgillivray, tailor, who has some time ago taken up his father's business. He keeps a large number of apprentices, and is indeed one of the best masters in town for teaching young men the trade. His customers mainly hail from the Leachkin and the Blackpark. Next door is a small tavern kept by Widow Macbean. Her twin sons, Jack and San, who are both tailors, have just had their evening meal, and are taking a stroll towards Friars' Shott fishing ground. Jack, as you will see, looks somewhat bronzed and weather-beaten, and his rolling seaman-like step smacks more of a ship's deck than of the tailor's board. He appears to be somewhat out of sorts. The reason is not far to seek. During the past

year or more his experiences have been quite as exciting as those of Robinson Crusoe.   In consequence of
his youthful thirst for adventure and his yearning for a
life on the ocean wave, he unfortunately "swallowed
the anchor," or, in other words, ran away to sea, and on
his return voyage from Buenos Ayres his ship took fire,
and he and the remainder of the survivors were for nine
days in an open boat, and afterwards cast ashore on an
almost desert island.   They were picked up by a Dutch
man-of-war, and after several months of untold hardship, Jack succeeded in again reaching the banks of the
Ness.   Having once more found himself under the
parental roof and back to the board, he asserts that
henceforth he will roam no more on the illimitable
watery wastes, and his seafaring will be confined to
crossing Kessock Ferry and the singing of an occasional
nautical song such as—

> " As we gather in a ring,
>   And with cheerful voices sing,
>   Oh, gaily goes the ship
>   When the winds blow fair."

The young men are joined by John Macpherson
("Heck"), who, as trade is rather quiet in town,
strongly advises the young men to go to Glasgow, that
city being the El Dorado of all aspiring young Highlanders.   A few paces further brings us to the river's
bank, where the salmon fishers, as you will notice, are
busily engaged plying their vocation, and as there is an
excellent run of fish at present, fair catches are made.
The people of this locality are much interested in the
fishing, as is indicated by the large crowd standing
around the nets eagerly watching the hauls.   The
season has not been by any means a successful one up
till now, but within the past week or two fish have
become more plentiful, and the lessee is making up for

lost time, although the most provoking part of the whole business is that a few days hence operations will have to cease, as close time will be on. Among the crowd of onlookers are many of the best known Green worthies, and had we been able to spare time we might have gone down and had a chat with them. We lingered too long, however, in the Foundry and on Wells Street, so we must therefore defer our visit for a day or two, when we will probably see them finish the season.

CHAPTER XVI.

FRIARS' SHOTT (*continued*).

As we arranged when last we met, we will now stroll
straight down to Friars' Shott, and as can be seen from
the crowds gathered there, exceptionally large hauls
are being obtained. Why, you can already see the fish
floundering and spluttering in the net there just as the
fishermen are dragging it ashore. That stout, robust-
looking gentleman, arrayed in frock coat and silk hat,
who in a clear treble east country accent is giving
directions to the fishermen, is Mr. Andrew Hutcheson,
the lessee of the fishings. He seems in excellent
humour to-day, and evidently anticipates to make up
during the next few days for his losses in the early part
of the season. Mr. Hutcheson, who is a prosperous
citizen, has an extensive auctioneering business, and is
altogether a thorough-going, shrewd, energetic business
man, of whom it may, with some degree of truth, be
said (to use a commonplace phrase) that he is " never
at rest but when he is over head and ears in work."
The two fishermen whom you see carrying up the
silvery beauties and placing them in the box are John
Fraser (" Balaam"), a native of the Leachkin, and Sandy
Maclennan, a well-known townsman, who are considered
two of the most expert fishermen on the waters of the
Ness. John, as you may gather from the authoritative
tone in which he addresses the other men, is looked upon
as the gaffer. A little further along, seated on the shingle,
is John Paterson, who, poor fellow, has unfortunately

lost a leg, which has been replaced by a wooden one.
He is at present, as you can see, busily engaged repairing the extra set of nets. In looking at Paterson, as he
deftly and diligently pursues his occupation, I am
reminded of a story of Lord Nelson, who upon one
occasion, while visiting a marine hospital, came upon
one of his gallant Jack tars, who, like himself, had lost
an arm in fighting his country's battles. Looking
pensively at his own empty sleeve and then at the
sailor, he quietly said, "I am afraid, Jack, they have
spoiled both of us for fishers." The loss of a leg, however, does not seem to have prevented Paterson from
mending his nets, nor yet, for that matter, does it hinder
him from fishing, for he is one of the most active men
in the squad. There is the coble coming down the
stream again, and as she cuts rapidly across so as to
prevent the fish getting clear of the net, the crowd
slowly step down to the edge of the stream. The rope
is attached to the "crab," and with much energy the
men wind away until the lower part of the net is
pulled ashore. All the fish that are within its meshes
are now secure. Slowly and methodically the men
pass it in hand-over-hand as they eagerly watch to see
if they have succeeded in making a haul this time.
Luck again! Don't you see the extraordinary commotion in the water, while the men step out into the
water and hold up the net a couple of feet above the
surface, in case some of the fish may escape? John
Fraser is looking around for his stick, which he has
now found, and as the "bag" of the net is hauled up
almost high and dry, he begins his work of destruction,
and—thud!—thump!—thud!—thirty splendid fish—
salmon, grilse, and sea trout—lie at his feet. The
unusual "take" is evidently the subject of comment
with the bystanders, prominent among whom is our

friend, Sergeant William Chisholm, one of the burgh
officers. Listen! he is just telling some of the crowd
that he can remember when he was a boy seeing cart-
loads of beautiful salmon landed at the Castle Shott,
which is on the east side of the river a few yards above
the stone bridge, and almost immediately below the
Castle Hill. Sandy Grant (" Supple ") is also looking on ;
he has just remarked, "How much of that fish, I wonder,
would be given to the poor?" Yes, the poor we have
always with us. Sandy, who is the terror of the local
law-breaker, is a kind, warm-hearted man, although by
virtue of his office he has ofttimes to assume a stern
exterior. His " bark is, however, worse than his bite."
Another conspicuous figure among the onlookers is our
old friend, Donald Treasurer, the well-known son of St.
Crispin from Davis Square, whom you will remember
we met at Muirtown Bridge some time ago, *en route*,
as he told us himself, for the Cape in search of a son.
He has, as we anticipated, returned ere he got the
length of that distant colony. By his side are other
two of his sons. One has recently got married, while
the other is seriously meditating taking a step in the
same direction, much to the satisfaction of the old man.
Donald, although well up in years, is brimful of humour,
and a spare hour spent in his workshop listening to his
yarns is a most amusing, if not instructive, pastime. He
is still as expert at his trade as in the days of his youth,
and it may be said that in that respect the entire
family take after him, as may be gathered from the
fact that they get Mr. Jack, the royal bootmaker's,
best work. Donald is also a great bird-fancier, and in
his own humble way has quite an aviary. He often
pays a visit to " the Double Dykes " with his calling
bird on the outlook for linnets, and he seldom returns
empty-handed. There is another brother in trade, Tom

Fraser ("Gow"), who with his leather apron strung around him has stepped down to the water's edge in order to enjoy a whiff of the pipe and a breath of the autumnal air. He is in conversation with another of the craft, Donald Dallas. Although interested in the extraordinary catch of fish, they seem, judging from the snatches of conversation which I can pick up, to be more concerned about the recent Chartist Riots in Manchester and Newport. Both are keen politicians and much interested in the progress of reform. That neatly-attired, intelligent-looking, middle-sized man who has just joined them is Mr. Lockhart Fraser, carpenter, Muirtown Street, who is accompanied by his two daughters, pretty little girls, of whom he is justly proud. He takes part in the "crack," which has now become quite animated. Mr. Fraser, who is a splendid mechanic and a most sociable man, is, along with his worthy spouse, held in high respect in the district. Seated on and standing around the salmon boxes are a group of well-known Green residenters, who seem much amused at some incident which is being related to them by Donald Mackintosh ("Dachan"), who in his own quaint way is quite a humorist. They are moving away now, and it can be easily seen that they are making a "bee-line" for "The Black Bull." The usual crowd is standing by the tavern door, evidently on the lookout for some one who will have the generosity to invite them inside and stand them a dram all round. That tall, respectable-looking man with the clean-shaven face and wearing the conventional silk hat whom you see going from door to door, book and pencil in hand, is Mr. George Macleod, tailor, who acts as officer of the West Church, and is one of the best-known and most respected men on the west side of the river. As the Rev. Mr. Clark has commenced his catechising, Mr. Macleod is soliciting

G

the names of those who will attend each evening. He usually obtains the promise of some individual members of the various families to attend the meeting in the church, when they will undergo an examination in the Catechism in either Gaelic or English, the church officer calling out the names from the steps of the lectern when their turn comes. The meetings are very popular, and the reverend gentleman spares no effort to make them as profitable as possible. We have stayed so long down among the salmon fishers that there is little time left to do the Green this evening, as antici- pated, and I think the better plan will be to return home and devote another evening to it, for it is a most interesting spot, and in taking a hurried run through it we would overlook many persons and points worthy of note.

CHAPTER XVII.

GREEN OF MUIRTOWN—DAVIS SQUARE—JOHN
MACLEAN'S STORY.

IT is a pleasant autumnal afternoon, and we find ourselves again in that interesting, I might almost say
classic, locality known as the Green of Muirtown, a
spot so dear to the heart of many Invernessians not only
at home but in far distant lands and 'neath alien skies.
The design of the buildings is, as you will observe, of a
somewhat crude nature, and in architectural beauty the
edifices may not equal many of the other buildings in
town, but their designers and builders apparently looked
more to comfort than elegance in their construction.
We are now on Muirtown Street, which was formerly
known as Beauly Street, it being the outlet of the town
to the Aird district. To the left is Mackintosh's Close,
through which, if you have no objection, we will take a
stroll. We are now in the vicinity of Davis Square.
It is not generally known, although it is nevertheless a
fact, that previous to the construction of the Caledonian Canal a small stream that runs down the face of
the Leachin and past the farm of Kinmylies meandered
down through the level fields of Muirtown and emptied
itself into the Ness at Friars' Shott. That fact is clearly
indicated by the names of the closes—Mill Lade and
Swan Lane—leading from Muirtown Street. There was,
no doubt, away back in the past, a meal mill at this
point, and its site was probably close to where Davis
Square now stands, while the dam would have most

likely been in the immediate locality. We have now
reached Duff Street, which, like Huntly Street, is called
after the proprietor, the genial and gentlemanly laird of
Muirtown. A few paces further along and we are in
Celt Street, where I observe three well-known residents
in conversation. One is Mr. Bisset, stoneware merchant,
Muirtown Street, whose place of business I already
pointed out to you. He is the descendant of a very
ancient family, who were once closely allied to the Frasers
of Lovat. The other is Mr. Colin Young, a well-known
knight of St. Crispin. One might imagine from his garb,
tall hat included, and the black bag which with a
professional air he carries in his hand, that he is an influential limb of the law on business bent. This receptacle, however, is merely used for carrying to his work
the indispensable " understandings " of his many
customers. He is an excellent tradesman, and is well
employed. The third party, that firmly-set, square-
shouldered man of short stature, is Mr. Robert Forbes,
ship carpenter, who has just returned from a long voyage.
He is evidently much pleased to have his feet on *terra
firma*, and to find himself among his old friends. He is,
as you will observe, quite loquacious, and is doubtless
spinning some yarn of his experiences in other lands.
The Homeland, however, is to him the dearest land on
earth, and the " Big Green " the fairest spot beneath the
sun. Further down the street you will observe other
two residenters. They are Sergeant Hay and Mr. Alexander Fraser, baker. Hark! Mr. Fraser is expressing
the wish that the Corn Law Repeal Bill will soon become
law, so that he may be able to provide a cheaper loaf
for his customers, who mostly belong to the working-
class, to whom bread means life itself. Let us fervently
re-echo his wish in this all-important matter, and trust
in Providence.

You ask who that aged man coming round the corner, leaning on his staff and on the arm of a younger man, is. You can see at a glance that he is one of the good old school by his garb—blue Kilmarnock bonnet, short coat, blue breeches, black stockings, shoes and buckles. That is John Maclean, who is now wearing on towards the century, and the young man is his grandson, who generally accompanies him. They are just going over to the riverside to have a seat on one of the salmon cases, as is their custom. Let us quietly go along and endeavour to get into conversation with the old man, whose memory is of a most retentive character, so that he is possessed of a rich store of native lore and interesting reminiscences. You just stand aside for a little and listen while I engage him in conversation. "How are you to-day, Mr. Maclean?" "Considering my great age, I have no reason to complain." "Am I correct in assuming, Mr. Maclean, that you were born about the time of Culloden?" "I was born in the parish of Wardlaw, or Kirkhill, on January 7th, 1746, just about three months before that ever-memorable battle. I was brought up a good deal with my grandfather, who was born a few years previous to the Revolution of 1688. Having received just a little schooling at the Parish School, I was sent to learn the tailoring with a country master, and used to have grand times going from farm to farm sewing the homespun cloth that my master cut into garments. Many a strange story I listened to at the ceilidhs during the long winter evenings in these country homes, stories weird and awful, that would make one feel very eerie indeed." "Did you come into the town often on these occasions, Mr. Maclean?" "Yes, pretty often, for little bits of things required for the trade, which could only be got in the town, and I can assure you I have seen many changes take place since I first

began to come to Inverness. The only shop in town
existing now that was known to me in my young days
was the wine shop. at the foot of Bridge Street. You
may easily understand that the town was quite a different place then to what it is now, there being only four
inhabited houses on this side of the river at that time.
They hadn't the same communication with the south
that they have now with their coaches and what not.
Do you know, I was over sixty years of age before the
first coach started to run between here and Perth. I
mind when 'Donald Scholar' was confined in the
dungeon below the footway of the bridge yonder, and I
can recollect seeing the boys dangling pieces of bread in
front of his lonely cell. He was very particular though,
and would rather have white bread than oat bannock.
I mind on one occasion, about the year 1790, being at
the east end of the town, when I was startled by hearing a tremendous noise which seemed to shake the whole
neighbourhood. I was not long in finding out that the
cause of it all was that the ruins of the old Castle on the
hill had fallen down the face of the brae, a portion of it
splashing into the river, the reason being that the elements had undermined the foundations." "How did
the people live at that time?" "Their mode of life
was very frugal indeed. Money was scarce, and the
necessaries of life were very difficult to obtain. Things
were not so bad in the town, fish being plentiful. I can
remember seeing a housewife getting from a fishwife as
many as forty-four haddocks for a sixpence, and so much
greed did she display, that she would not close the bargain
until she got the forty-fifth. In the country food was
composed principally of brose and kail, and as a luxury
for supper 'brochan sneap,' with the addition of a small
piece of butter. About the New Year time we could
generally manage a gill or two of whisky (big measure)

to wash these delicacies down. There was no fear of
the people dying then from being overfed. The cloth-
ing of the men and women was generally homespun
material from wool grown on the farm or croft, and dyed
with 'crotal.' We tailors used to get a few pence a day
and our food for our work. They were always very
careful to give us a good bed, and generally treated us
handsomely as their means would admit." "Have you
been able to do any work recently?" "Yes, until a few
years ago. I used to make clothes for Mr. Baillie of
Dochfour and some of his friends. Indeed, about the
last job I made, however, was this pair of breeches for
myself which I am now wearing. I sent them round
to Mr. Macgillivray to put button-holes on, as my eye-
sight is failing, but I think I could have made a better
job myself." "You like to stroll about still?" "Oh,
yes, my grandson helps me about nicely, and I like very
much to go and hear my dear minister, Mr. Clark, on
Sundays." "Well, we'll be bidding you good evening,
Mr. Maclean. You have seen many changes in your
day?" "Ay, many changes." What do you think of
that interesting old gentleman, now? Isn't he brimful
of reminiscences, and altogether a source of great interest.
We have lingered so long talking to him that we must
now get away home, as it is getting on to tea time.
Hark! there is Wells' Foundry bell just announcing the
hour of six.

NOTE.—The person who gave the name to Davis
Square was a Welshman, who came to Inverness early
in the last century in connection with the construction
of the Caledonian Canal. He was for many years well
known as an amateur farmer, in which calling he was
not successful. At one time he had a fruit garden in
the vicinity of the Square, and being somewhat par-

simonious, he used to get the Green boys to pick the
berries for him, but he made it a condition that while
doing so they would require to be whistling to evidence
that they were doing their work properly.   John Maclean, to whom we have referred in the foregoing chapter,
was for many years an outstanding character in town,
and had many friends to whom he was always ready to
converse with on the subject of bygone times, tales of
which he had an ample store.   Mr. Bond, of the *Inverness
Herald*, edited a small volume, containing his reminiscences, which is very interesting, and is still sought
after.   In 1848 he became the recipient of a gratuity
from the late Queen Victoria.   The old man was very
partial to a walk along the river side, sometimes going
the length of the Infirmary accompanied by one of his
grandsons.   He was only a few days laid aside when
the end came, and still possessing his faculties to a remarkable degree, he asked his attendant, " What day of
the month is this ? "   On being told that it was the 6th
of January 1851, he replied, " Well, if I live till to-
morrow I will complete my 105th year."   He did live
till four in the morning.   The good old man was interred in Greyfriars' Burying-Ground, the burial place
for centuries of the families of Baillie and Maclean.

CHAPTER XVIII.

CELT STREET—HUNTLY STREET—DISPENSARY.

WE meet again this afternoon at the foot of Celt Street, our intention being to continue our walk in the neighbouring locality. The weather is just a little threatening, yonder leaden clouds through which the sun peeps but dimly indicating that the flood-gates may open. Let us hope, however, that the rain will not descend until we have finished our stroll. That stout, amiable-looking gentleman who has just passed us and bade us "good day" is Mr. George Mackenzie, bootmaker, Church Street, who is on his way to his place of business from his residence in Muirtown Street. The young man accompanying him is his son William, who has just entered the business. Mr. Mackenzie has a number of sons to whom he is desirous of imparting a liberal education, in order to equip them for the battle of life. He is himself one of the good old school, whose motto is "Live and let live." As a churchman he is much attached to the Establishment, and is an elder in the West Parish Church. Standing in that doorway on the right hand side of the street, talking to his mother, is Captain Brotchie, the master of the trading schooner "Stirling Castle," just returned from a voyage to North Shields. The captain is well known throughout all the British ports as a Methodist local preacher, and never misses an opportunity of preaching the Gospel, while at the same time he makes a point of diffusing temperance principles. As showing his zeal, I may say that several

years ago, while visiting the Shetland Islands, he
observed a lack of Gospel teaching among the people,
and on his return he represented the state of affairs to
the Methodist conference, with the result that they
subsequently deputed Dr. Adam Clark to visit the
islands for the purpose of founding a mission. This
pioneer of Methodism received an excellent reception,
and the mission is now in a prosperous state. Although
a native of Dingwall, Captain Brotchie may not inaptly
be termed a citizen of the world, for he is ubiquitous,
and is indeed at home in every port into which he sails.
That smart, sharp-eyed lad who has just stepped up and
shaken him by the hand is his nephew, Willie Ferguson,
who is the popular leader of youthful sports and pas-
times in "The Green." Anything that he proposes in
the way of sport to his companions is always heartily
carried out. Indeed, if the old adage, "the boy is
father of the man," be true, he may yet become a leader
of men. That tall, thoughtful-looking gentleman in
clerical garb who is just standing at the Manse gate
on Muirtown Street is the Rev. Alexander Munro,
of the Queen Street Secession Church. The reverend
gentleman's kind-heartedness and genuine sympathy,
not merely with his own flock in Queen Street Church,
but with the people throughout the whole neighbourhood, has made him most popular. Not only is he
unwearied in his attention to their spiritual needs,
but he also sees to their material wants, and he is
therefore looked upon as an ideal minister. He
is always ready to help the down-trodden and the
oppressed, while, in the words of Goldsmith, " to relieve
the wretched is his pride." That gentleman who has
just gone up to him there is Donald Jack, slater, who
is a proprietor in a small way in King Street. There
is a good story told of him to the effect that, while pay-

ing his feu recently to Major Duff, he suggested that if he got Kenny Beaton's feu, which was next to his own, he could build on it, and thereby improve the amenities of the locality. The major, who was a bit of a humorist, although not much of a poet, immediately picked up a slip of paper, and with his quill penned the lines—

> " Here goes in a crack
> Kenny's feu to Donald Jack."
>
> *H. R. Duff.*

This conveyance was subsequently adjudged in Inverness Sheriff Court to be quite legal. We will now retrace our steps, and we find ourselves once again on Huntly Street. That building just beyond Mr. Fraser the baker's is the dispensary for the sick poor, as is indicated by the sign above the door-way. The laboratory is in charge of Mr. Stewart, tailor, who is most attentive to patients and visitors. The three gentlemen who have just stepped out of the front door are Dr. William W. Forbes, his brother Dr. George Forbes, and Mr. John Russell, slater, who have been attending a Board meeting. Mr. Russell, who is a native of the good town of Forres, came to Inverness, while yet a young man, and along with Dr. William Forbes had the credit in 1832 of founding the dispensary which has proved so great a boon to the suffering poor in town. Drs. George and William Forbes are two sons of a numerous family, their father being Dr. Forbes, who was for many years surgeon of the Inverness-shire Militia, a post which he held in addition to his local practice. On their mother's side they are grandsons of Mr. William Welsh, proprietor of Millburn, who was Provost of Inverness about the year 1790. The younger man, Dr. George, has just received his University diploma, and is about to sail for India to fulfil an important appointment in the East India Company's service. You will have observed that we passed King Street, on a portion of which was the old site of the "Kirk on the Green." Tradition tells us that at that point was situated a small chapel, where James IV. of Scotland worshipped during his visits to the Highlands (viz., in 1493-4, twice in 1499, in 1501, and 1503), and it was subsequently known as the King's Chapel, hence the name King Street. The adjoining street is appropriately called Queen Street, while the street upon which we now stand is known as Princes Place, a trio of royalties. Overhead you will observe three golden balls, which are said to have been the arms of the merchants of Lombardy, but are now popularly known as "mine uncle's" sign. A glance at the shop underneath indicates the business carried on. The genial proprietor is Mr. John Reeves, who, as you will observe, has a canvas bag attached to his waist. That is the cash-bag, in which there is usually a plentiful supply of silver and copper. He is always ready to give fourpence or sixpence in return for the "smoothing iron" or the potato chapper, which often enables the house-wife to get a dinner of potatoes and herring for the bairns till the father gets his pay. There is "Rob the Goat" from the Haugh with a small parcel in a coloured handkerchief making for the shop. He is just talking to Bailie Mackenzie ("London Boot"). Listen! what is that Bailie Mackenzie is saying to him? "Ah, Rob, are you not ashamed to be going to the pawn?" "No, Bailie," Rob is emphatically answering, "I am needing a little help, and this enables me to get what I require; but, Bailie, if I had nothing to pawn I might then be ashamed." He now hurries up, as he is evidently anxious to get the money at once for some specific purpose. Ah, the rain is now beginning to fall, and if we do not get home quickly we may reckon on wet jackets. In our next stroll we will start at Balnain House and continue northward.

Note.—Mrs. Brotchie, who is referred to above, lived to the advanced age of ninety-five. Her son, Captain Brotchie, was for many years chaplain of the Sailor's Bethel in Greenock, where he did a great work, and was latterly known as the Rev. Donald Brotchie. He was married four times, and lived to a patriarchal age. Captain Brotchie's nephew, William Ferguson, was one of the first volunteers in town, and afterwards turned out one of the finest shots in the country, winning the St. George's Vase at Wimbledon in 1860, and being at the same time almost successful in carrying away the Queen's Prize. He subsequently won many trophies, and rose to the rank of colonel in his battalion. Of the Rev. Alexander Munro, Queen Street Church, much could be said did space permit. "This eminent divine," says his biographer, "was a native of Kildonan, Sutherlandshire. On his outset in life he learned the painter business, at which he for some time wrought in Edinburgh. In the years 1814 and 1815 he acted as precentor in the Gaelic Church there to the Rev. Mr. Macdonald, afterwards of Ferrintosh. In 1820, when the union of the Secession Churches took place, he regularly attended their devotions, and was induced to leave the Established Church and join with them. Conceiving him eminently qualified for the ministry he was sent to college, and was licensed in 1824, being sent north shortly afterwards, Inverness, Dingwall, and Bridge of Dulsie being allotted as his stations. In 1833 he was ordained, and in 1836 inducted in Inverness, where he remained till his lamented death in 1855 at the age of sixty-seven. His manner in the

pulpit was lively and engaging, his sermons clear,
forcible, and convincing, shedding a lustre upon
every subject which he handled.   In catechising and in
visiting and administering consolation to the sick and
dying he excelled."   Of many anecdotes of him we record the following:—After being settled in the north
for some time he met his old friend, Dr. Macdonald,
who, being in a sarcastic mood, said to him, "Well,
Sandy, I hear you are turned preacher.   Where have
you left the brushes?"   With characteristic meekness
Mr. Munro answered, "Just where Peter left his nets."
"The Apostle of the North" was rebuked.   Dr. George
F. Forbes, another gentleman alluded to in this chapter
returned from India after an absence of thirty years,
and took up his residence in this country.   He handsomely endowed the dispensary, which is now known as
the Forbes Dispensary.

CHAPTER XIX.

QUEEN STREET—CENTRAL SCHOOL—PRINCES PLACE—
BLUE HOUSE—WEST CHURCH.

As the weather this afternoon is very much more pleasant than when we last visited the locality, I feel sure that our present walk will be a more enjoyable one, as we have many interesting personages and places to see. You will remember that when we last met we arranged to make Balnain House (Huntly Street) our starting-point, but, before our inspection of it, let us retrace our steps and cover some of the ground which we traversed last week. We will first take a glance at Queen Street, which, you will notice, is in a somewhat unfinished state, gaunt, bare walls standing out here and there as an eyesore to the public, so that to those who have no eye for the antique it might probably give very much the same impression as the ruins of ancient Rome did to the Highlander who visited the Seven Hills, when he was constrained to exclaim that " Rome wud be a fine city if it wass wance finished." We will now turn towards the Central School, which, as I think I already told you, is under the supervision of Bell's Trustees, composed of the Town-Council and the parish ministers. The scholars are just being dismissed, and that stout, dark gentleman who has just come out of the front door is Mr. John Douglas, the master, who came to Inverness from Stirling a few years ago. In consequence of his complexion being somewhat of the same hue of the children of Ham, the scholars bestowed upon him the familiar nickname of "Blaka," which gives him not the slightest offence. He is much beloved by his pupils, the majority of whom, unlike average school children, seem to take a special delight in attending his classes. This is clearly evident from the alacrity with which they may be seen making for the school in the morning in response to the "ting-a-ling-ting-a-lingle!" of the bell, which is interpreted by them to mean—

"Come, scholars, come, scholars, to Blackaman's School,
   He's neither a hard man nor is he a fool."

It is nothing unusual to hear groups of scholars sing this in chorus as, books and slate in hand, they hurry along Queen Street in the morning. Mr. Douglas is one of the most painstaking and successful teachers that ever was in the north, as many who passed through his hands can amply testify. A strict disciplinarian, he will brook no scheming, while at the same time the scholar who evinces a desire to increase his knowledge is gently dealt with. Mr. Douglas has just observed us, and beckoned us to step inside, so we will follow him into the school. "Good morning, Mr. Douglas. You have a large attendance of lads and lasses under your tuition." "Yes, and I have not the slightest doubt but that many of them will yet attain prominence in the various walks of life, for the majority of them are apt scholars, whom any master might be proud of having the honour of teaching. I am endeavouring to introduce the latest methods in teaching, and I am glad to find that my efforts are appreciated by the scholars, thus making a pleasure of what in other circumstances might prove a disappointing task." "You believe, Mr. Douglas, that there is still room for improvement in existing educational matters?" "Oh, certainly, but that will all come in the course of time. For instance, look at the great improvement within recent years. Not so very long ago the art of writing was taught by means of shallow boxes containing sand, and smoothed over with a small ruler. On this surface the letters were formed by means of the forefinger. The slate was the next stage, and now we have got the copybook. Here is a specimen of one of my scholar's writing, which you will, I think, admit is very creditable, considering the fact that the lad is only a beginner. The elder scholars are learned in map-drawing and the use of the globes, and occasionally get instruction in music, while a smattering of Latin is also taught." "We will now bid you good afternoon, Mr. Douglas, as it is unfair to detain you after the day's work is over, and can only thank you for your courtesy." We will step further along the street. That building on the left, just beyond the school, is the Rev. Alexander Munro's church, which, although comparatively small, accommodates the congregation. Among that group of lads standing on the opposite side of the street are Lachlan and Roderick Kemp, Colin Jack, and Alick Macphail, four boys who, by their frolicsome and lively natures, keep their youthful companions in amusement. The top of Queen Street is now reached, and yonder across the fields you can see the newly-arrived steamer at Muirtown letting off steam. Standing beside the porch of that cottage to the left is Mr. Murdo Macleod, mason, who, along with a fellow-elder, Mr. Macleod, lamplighter, is holding a conversation with their esteemed pastor, the Rev. Mr. Munro. You ask me what that fortress-like wall to the left is. That is the back wall of the garden of Balnain House, which, by-the-by, I had almost forgotten. We will now step round to the front, as, not being sons of Anak, we cannot

possibly see over the wall. Standing in his doorway
there in Princes Place is Mr. Caird, a gentleman who
is in the commission business in town. It may interest
you to know that in conversation with Mr. Caird some
time ago he informed me that he witnessed the last
execution for sheep stealing in Scotland, which took
place at Aberdeen many years ago. We have now
reached the Balnain coachman and gardener's house.
The big house itself is occupied by Captain Fraser of
Balnain and family. The Captain himself is at present
abroad. The mansion, as you can see, is not notable
for the beauty of its architecture. Its whole outline
is in fact painfully plain, with the exception of the
portico in front, the pillars evidently being intended to
represent marble, although in reality they are only
wood. The house is said to have been erected towards
the close of the last century by a retired indigo planter,
and was in consequence known for many years as the
"Blue House." It used to be copied or sewn by the
Inverness lassies on their "samplers" as an ideal
mansion, and it is possible that some of these may be
still in existence. It is to be hoped that in the course
of time that huge wall which surrounds it will be
removed, as it is entirely out of place in a working-class
locality. Indeed, it is quite possible that ere many
years will have passed such a change will take place.
That sacred edifice adjoining the wall on the south side
is the West Parish Church, which has been recently
erected by the collegiate minister, the Rev. Alexander
Clark, who, on becoming aware of the needs of this
quarter of the town, obtained the money for its construction. The front presents an excellent specimen of Ionic
architecture, and the huge building itself is seated for
1800 persons, while at the back there is a session-house,
vestry, and other offices. At the west end there was to

have been erected a handsome spire, but for lack of
funds the building had to be finished off with a small
wooden dome or cupola, which contains an excellent
bell. The door being open, we will take a look in.
The excellent manner in which the woodwork is finished
is worthy of notice, as is also the oak graining of the
sides and ceiling, while over the pulpit you will observe
a scroll bearing the words, "We preach Christ crucified."
The entire painting of the interior was executed by
Mr. James Shepherd, painter, Petty Street, who is one
of the leading decorators in town. The neat and substantial railing which encloses the front of the church
is a striking contrast to the unsightly wall we have
just passed. We are now on the roadway again. There
is evidently some special church meeting just about to
be held, as I can see the trim, neat figure of Bailie
Maclean, Dochgarroch, coming down the riverside
towards the gate. He is now joined by Lachlan
Mackintosh of Raigmore, who is accompanied by his son,
Eneas William, whom he generally brings along with
him to all public functions. It is the laird's great
ambition that the young man should become an
advocate, nay, even rise to the loftiest legal position.
Did you overhear that remark which Bailie Maclean
has just made to Raigmore regarding the feu rent of
£26, which he maintains is too much, while the latter
is referring him to the grand church which they have
got? Yonder is the stately and portly figure of the Rev.
Mr. Clark, the esteemed pastor of the congregation,
coming in sight. As he comes nearer, we will have a
better opportunity of seeing him. The face, which is
of a strong intellectual caste, the clear complexion, the
steady eye, and the stately bearing bespeak a man
among men, and if any man ever deserved the desig-
nation of "reverend" Mr. Clark is that one. We will,

I think, cease from our wanderings this afternoon,
as we have other business to attend to, but we will
again resume where we left off. We have perhaps
not been able to get over very much ground, but I think
you will admit that our short ramble has not been altogether uninteresting.

NOTE.—With regard to my reference to Mr. Douglas
in this chapter, it may not be out of place to
mention the names of three prominent local writing-
masters of bygone times. Mr. Willam Macculloch, who
succeeded Mr. Picton in the Central School in 1829,
was considered one of the finest caligraphists of his
time. I had the pleasure of seeing a beautiful specimen
of his writing in the shop of the late Mr. Forbes, painter,
Academy Street, who was an old friend of his. After
being in several situations in England, he was latterly
writing-master in the Academy at Fleetwood. Some
time after Mr. Macculloch left the Central School Mr.
Douglas became master, and, as I have already said,
put a number of pupils through his hands, many of
whom hold important positions, among whom I may
mention Sheriff Davidson, Fort-William, Mr. Henry
Mitchell, chemist, Union Street, and Mr. William
Mackenzie, Huntly Street. While Mr. Douglas was a
good all-round teacher, he excelled as a writing-master.
It is worthy of record that Mr. Douglas was a great
favourite with and took great interest in the out-door
sports engaged in by his pupils. Particularly in
teaching them the useful art of swimming (an art in
which the young men of Inverness held the record for
many years). He was married to Miss Wells, a daughter
of Mr. Wells of the Foundry. Mr. Douglas was
offered a better position in Dollar, to which town he
removed in July of that year, much to the regret of his

scholars and a wide circle of friends. After being for a number of years there he retired, and died a few years ago considerably over ninety years of age. He and his worthy spouse were always glad to have a visit from any of their old Inverness pupils. Mr. Falconer, late of the Royal Academy, was another notable writing-master. He came to Inverness in search of manual labour, which he obtained, but he discovered that he could write a very fine commercial hand of writing, and he accordingly took rooms in a thatched house on High Street, on the present site of the British Linen Company's Bank, and pupils flocked to him. On a vacancy occurring in the Academy he was at once engaged, which position he held for a lengthened period. The Rev. Mr. Clark, West Parish Church, to whom I also referred, first saw the light in Inverness in 1797. After having passed a successful curriculum and taken his degree, he was inducted in 1820 as colleague with Mr. Rose, afterwards Dr. A very considerable amount of the work of the parish devolved upon Mr. Clark, who was indefatigable in his ministrations, and in him the poor found a constant friend. Indeed, he looked upon the poor as his special charge. He observed the necessity for a Parish Church on the west side of the river in 1840. At that time dissent from the Establishment was in the air, yet, notwithstanding this, Mr. Clark proceeded with the building of the church. Although at first feeling disposed to join the Disruption party, he followed the advice of his friends, and remained with the Establishment. This considerably impaired his ministerial work. The reverend gentleman was a theologian and classical scholar of a very high order, and his pulpit eloquence was such as to command close attention from his hearers. During the progress of the Poor Law Bill he constantly advocated that the rates should fall upon the moneyed classes. Later on an attempt was made to absorb the Mackintosh Farr Fund in consequence of the scarcity of pupils. Mr. Clark went on several occasions to the Court of Session, and in eloquent terms protested against such being done, and elicited the commendation of the Court, one judge remarking that he did not think there was such an advocate in the north, while another said that if he had made the bar his choice instead of the pulpit he would have become one of the most powerful legal luminaries that Scotland ever produced. Owing to constant work and increasing anxiety his health broke down, and in 1852 he went to Rothesay to recruit, but, alas! without avail, and in March of that year he passed away. He was universally mourned. In the words of the poet—

> "His life was gentle, and the elements
> So mixed in him that nature might stand up
> And say to all the world, 'This was a man.'"

He was buried in the Chapelyard, his funeral being perhaps the largest that ever was seen in the north of Scotland. He left a widow and daughter and two sons Henry died in India while yet a young man; Alexander, who held a situation in the London and County Bank, died in March 1904.

CHAPTER XX.

HUNTLY STREET (*continued*).

We have again met to continue our "daunder" through the Capital. It is now a considerable time since we set out on our exploration of the ancient and royal burgh, but, as I do not believe in rushing things of this kind, I have not conducted you through it at a break-neck pace, preferring rather to "do" the town by easy stages, while at the same time noting and explaining, to the best of my ability, everything of interest along our path. While we have now traversed a considerable part of the town, there is, I need hardly tell you, some interesting ground to get over yet, and I trust that in our few remaining walks I will be able to interest you even more so than I have done during those we have completed. We meet this afternoon where we parted company the other evening—in front of the West Parish Church— and just in passing I might mention that, in my opinion, the planting of a few trees in front of it would improve the amenities of the locality very considerably. That tall, handsome, dignified-looking gentleman standing on the roadway there in front of his dwelling awaiting his wife and beautiful daughter, who are coming out at the front door, is collector Cormick, who is the chief Inland Revenue officer in the district. Do you know when I see him I am always reminded of Prince Jerome Bonaparte, nephew of the Great Napoleon, the resemblance is so remarkably striking. Next door is the residence of Alexander Macdonald, wine merchant, whom I

already pointed out to you, as you will remember, down
at the Tanyard.   The adjoining cottage is occupied by
Mr. George Macleod, tailor, the respected and popular
officer of the West Church.   He has a wonderful
collection of pets, for, being a religious man, he believes
with Coleridge that " he prayeth best who loveth best
all things both great and small."   Let us step in and
see Mr. Macleod, while at the same time we will have
an opportunity of getting a glimpse of his live stock.
I will just knock at the door.   Here he comes.   " Oh,
how are you, Mr. Macleod ?   I have taken the liberty
of calling round with my friend so that he might have
a look at your pets."   " I'm pretty well, thank you.
Come right in.   This is the monkey, ' Jacko,' the little
scoundrel.   He is not a beauty, as you can see at a
glance, but what he lacks in looks he makes up for in
wit.   He was given to my son by Sween Macdonald,
Clachnaharry, who brought him home from the East
Indies during one of his voyages.   The little animal is
remarkably 'cute, and I will now put him through some
of his tricks.   Having seen him, you must admit that
he has wonderful instinct, call it intelligence if you
will.   I haven't learned him to sew yet, but he is not
without his use, for as a saver of fuel he cannot be excelled, and that means something in these hard times.
It is his delight to sit on the hearth all day and replace
the cinders in the fire, so that not even the smallest
piece is lost until it is consumed to ashes.   Now, ' Jacko,'
make your bow to the gentlemen.   (Bows.)   Could any
member of Her Majesty's service come to the salute
with more exact military precision than that ?   This is
my favourite dog, ' Dash,' a Scotch terrier.   ' Jacko ' and
he are great friends, although they are both pretty bad-
tempered.   He is also able to go through certain performances.   Come, ' Dash ' (performs certain tricks).

What do you think of that now?" "Where is your 'blackie,' Mr. Macleod? I often hear him sing as I pass." "Oh, 'Charlie,' the scamp; he is over in the gardens on the other side of the river. I let him out every day, but I'll call him. Here he comes flying across. Come on, you little rascal, where have you been all the afternoon? Get into your cage there. Don't be alarmed at the door swinging open like that, it's only the pigeon which I have taught to admit itself by undoing the 'sneck.' This is 'Tom,' the cat, which has just entered. Strange to say, they all agree wonderfully, although 'Jacko' would like to have the mastery, but his right is ofttimes disputed by 'Tom' and 'Dash.'" "Thank you, Mr. Macleod, very much for showing us your most interesting collection. We are detaining you from your business, and will now bid you good afternoon." That was a most interesting visit, was it not? and there are few more intelligent men than Mr. Macleod. I may mention that his father was in the Peninsular War, and returned home invalided. Mr. Macleod is always willing to render assistance and advice to those requiring help. That sacred edifice is the Catholic Chapel (St. Mary's). You will observe that the design is perpendicular Gothic. It has been erected in place of the former chapel, which was on Margaret Street. The interior has been rather crudely frescoed with Scriptural scenes by an artist from Fochabers named Russell, if I mistake not, at three shillings per square yard. The altar-piece, which depicts Peter receiving the keys from our Lord, is on the whole a painting of some merit. As compared with the West Church, the feu-duty is remarkably small, viz., 1s. 3d. from the frontage right back to King Street. At the front door, in semi-canonicals, is Father Mackenzie, to whom we would fain ascribe the piety of Saint Francis of

Assisi, or the enthusiasm of Savonarola, but we pass on.
We are now in front of David Fraser's ("Davy Ginger")
grocery establishment. He is just talking to Mr. Macdonald of the Tanyard, who, as I already told you, is a
member of the Catholic communion. He is just saying,
" I am surprised, Mr. Macdonald, that you are connected
with that Catholic religion "; while Mr. Macdonald
smilingly replies, " You are short-sighted in any case,
Mr. Fraser, but you are particularly so in regard to this
matter." We will step along, and have now reached the
shop and dyehouse of Mr. Young, dyer. This industry is
one which was at one time most flourishing in the town,
but is now fast dying out. These dyeworks have been
held by the family for several generations. Formerly
there was a toll of $\frac{1}{2}$d. per passenger on the stone bridge
over there, and the country people from the Redcastle
district were exempted from paying the toll, but ere they
were allowed to pass they had to present a permit from
Mr. Murdo Young, which simply consisted of a slip of
paper on which the letter " Y " was inscribed by him.
That grocer's shop next door is kept by Mr. and Mrs.
Ross, a worthy couple, who are much respected in the
neighbourhood, and who are said to keep a good dram.
Close by is the shop of Mr. Matheson, baker, who keeps
excellent bread, and is much thought of by his many
customers. That tidy little body who is conversing
with Mrs. Matheson at the close-mouth is the widow of
John Macleod, an Inverness soldier, who married her
during the occupation of Portugal by the British army.
She is a Portugese lady, and her maiden name was
Mary Lopaz. She has brought up a family, and has
evidently not been able to return to her native sunny
south, although she never tires of dilating on its many
and varied beauties. A little farther on is another
old-established dyeworks, Mr. Andrew Logan's. In

the river are dyers washing out the yarn, prominent among whom is "John the Hielanman," while Mr. Macpherson ("Cluny"), the foreman, is superintending operations. Mr. Logan is, of course, busily engaged inside folding the newly dyed cloth. That leather shop is Mr. Alexander Fraser's establishment. A number of cronies generally foregather at this place. Among them may be found occasionally Murdo Graham, popularly known as "Tailair Tasdan" (the shilling tailor), his charges seldom exceeding that amount. See, they are there now. From what I overhear I can learn that they are discussing the persecutions of the Covenanters, and the atrocities of Graham of Claverhouse is mentioned. "Tailair Tasdan," who is evidently not well up in history, volubly asserts that it was utterly impossible that any man bearing the name of Graham could be guilty of such barbarities. He takes it very ill that it should be thought that a namesake of his was such a monster, and see, he has just left the shop in a towering rage. A door or two further on and we are at the residence of Mr. Munro, pumpmaker. There are his worthy helpmate, Mrs. Munro, and himself at the close, and the bright lad who approaches them smilingly with his satchel of books under his arm is their younger son, Henry. We are now in the vicinity of the Bridge, and as I see by the clock on the old steeple that tea time is approaching, we will adjourn on this occasion to meet again at the foot of King Street, with a view to making our way southward.

NOTE.—As we observed in a former chapter, Mr. George Macleod was for many years officer of the West Church, and his devoted services were highly appreciated by the kindly pastor, Mr. Clark. Mr. Macleod's eldest son, Alexander, served his apprenticeship with

Mr. Donald M'Culloch, draper, and in the summer of
1854 emigrated to Australia, and became one of the
pioneers of the colony of Victoria, and is now a resident
of the city of Melbourne. His second son, John, served
for several years in the office of Mr. Dallas, solicitor,
but subsequently joined the 38th Regiment, and served
in the Crimea and the Indian Mutiny. His youngest
son, George, was for many years a highly respected
clerk in the Inverness Post Office. Mr. Macleod died
in 1878.

CHAPTER XXI.

KING STREET.

As the nights are now beginning to fall, I thought it best that we should meet a little earlier this afternoon than has been our custom recently, so as to enable us to finish our walk before the "shades of eve begin to fall." We decided when last we met to resume our journey of exploration at the foot of King Street, and at that particular spot we now find ourselves. As we step along we may expect to meet not a few citizens who take no mean part in the battle of life. Why, there is one just coming along. A glance at the firmly-set figure, with professional air and wearing the conventional frock-coat and silk hat, is sufficient to reveal the fact that the gentleman is a medical man, and that he is evidently on his daily rounds among his patients. He is none other that Dr. Walker, a well-known local practitioner, whose skill has secured for him a large and growing practice. See, there he has just entered that house, where his presence will, I doubt not, be as a ray of hope to some sufferer within. That ramshakle, tarred wooden shed is the killing establishment of Angus Calder, flesher, Castle Street, and as I see there are several fleecy victims inside, I take it that an execution will in a short time take place. These youths you see gathered round are waiting with keen expectancy to see "Dunk," who assumes the *rôle* of killer, carry out his operations. "Dunk" is the proprietor's brother, and as his business capacity is not equal to that of Angus, this is the part of the business that suits him best. That consequential-looking man you see coming along is Mr. Calder, and he is apparently giving certain instructions to his brother, who has come out of the shed. He has now given his instructions to "Dunk," and is shouting on "Ian Scholar" to go over to the shop for his paper, as he likes a read in the afternoon. That is "Ian" who has rushed out from the centre of the group of boys, and without once looking behind, is making for Castle Street with the speed of a roebuck, while "Dunk" is shouting after him that, as a recompense, he will get some puddings to take home on his return. You will observe that he holds in his hand with a firm grasp not a banner on which is inscribed the word "Excelsior," but a board upon which a copy of the alphabet is pasted, which he has been trying to master since his infancy without any very great prospect of ever getting as far as X, Y, Z without a blunder, although his mother, whose only language is the vernacular, often says, "Tha Ian a' fas na sgoilear math le a leabhar-maide" (John is getting a good scholar with his wooden book). "Dunk" is now getting the killing stool out, and the boys are gathering closer, but as we have no desire to witness the "slaughtering of the innocents," we will pass on. We have now reached the residence of Mr. Murdo Mackenzie, plasterer, who along with his handsome wife is having a breath of air. Mr. Mackenzie, who is a most affable man, is in many respects a useful member of the community. He is a member of the local fire brigade, as you can see from the fact that his helmet, coat, and key hang conspicuously in the lobby, and he is ready to go on duty at a moment's notice. We are now directly behind the West Church, and you are doubtless anxious to know what that ruinous-looking building to the left is. It was said to have been originally used by the Lovat family as stables, and latterly it was turned into a brewery. A few years ago brewery operations within its walls were given up, and gradually it fell into ruins. We are now opposite the residence of our old friend, Sergeant Chisholm of the Burgh Police, who is just coming out of his door to resume duty after dinner. " Good afternoon, Sergeant ; you have a nice place here, and your supply of spring water from the well there is most convenient. It's a pity there are not more such cottages as yours in the neighbourhood." " There would be if the feus were not so high." You may well ask who that miserable, starved-looking creature clothed in rags is that has just entered the adjoining cottage. That is " Hustean, the Miser," who is making his way to his comfortless, cheerless garret. Little do those who look upon the old man with commiseration think that he usually carries on his person enough money which, if properly utilised, would keep him in comfort for the remainder of his days. We have got as far as the Factory Close now. The building, as you will notice, is divided into tenements, and from its appearance internally I should say that it was originally intended as a better-class dwelling. It is at present occupied by several handloom weavers, who carry on their work on the premises. They make serge and wincey for homewear. One of the principal occupants is Mr. Davidson, who is a most industrious man. His eldest son, Donald, who is just coming along the street, is employed in Mr. Belford's law office on High Street; while Alick, the younger son, is just returning from the Central School. There is Hugh Macleod, another tenant, coming out for his afternoon stroll. He is accompanied by George, the son of his old age. They

are on their way to contemplate nature beneath the
shade of the elm trees by the riverside. George is a
regular chip of the old block. Behind the close, in one
of a row of cabins, lives a well-known character nicknamed "Johon" (John Macdonald, tailor). He is
addicted to strong drink, poor fellow, and many a
weary vigil his old mother has kept while waiting his
return in the small hours of the morning. Let us now
step along. Standing in front of his house there is Mr.
Austin, professor of dancing. His graceful figure indicates his profession. He is conversing with his son,
James, a smart lad, who has just put in his books after
returning from school. Mr. Austin is a painter of
considerable merit, and his spare time is occupied in
pursuing the art. Almost opposite is the residence of
Mr. Noble, cartwright, Castle Street, to whom I already
referred. Seated in that gig, which is being driven
westward, is Mr. John Phillip, R.S.A., who is on his
way to his cottage at Divach, Glen-Urquhart. That
small meal shop is the by-no-means pretentious business place of Marsali Ruadh (or "Red May," as the young
people call her). When "May" is not engaged in
dealing out the meal she usually spends the time
sitting on a low stool by the fireside poring over her
well-worn Bible, and would indeed make an excellent
subject for John Phillip, whom we have just seen, for
a picture entitled, "Preparing for the Promised Land."
Mr. Cameron's inn is on the opposite side. There he
is standing inside the doorway, and he is to my mind
a typical boniface, bluff and jovial. The provision
shop at the corner is occupied by Mr. and Mrs. Fraser,
who are assisted in their business by their family.
They came from Nairn some years ago and settled in
town, where they are held in high respect for their
many good qualities. We have now reached the head

of King Street, and will cease for the day. On the next occasion on which we meet I will endeavour to describe Tomnahurich Street, with special reference to some of its inhabitants.

NOTE.—Many years subsequent to the date of which I write, poor John Macdonald (" Johon ") became, alas! like many others, a victim to the Ness, his remains being washed ashore at Kilmuir. He was interred in the burying-ground there by several kind friends, who defrayed the expenses. His grave is still pointed out.

CHAPTER XXII.

TOMNAHURICH STREET.

IF I remember correctly, we agreed to start our pere-
grinations this afternoon from this particular point (the
south end of King Street), for the purpose of having a
look at Tomnahurich Street and some of the interesting
buildings and personages in the locality. I may explain at the outset that the street is called after Tomnahurich Hill, which is situated three-quarters of a
mile distant. The name is said to be a Gaelic one, the
meaning of which is the Hill of the Boat. It is sometimes known as the Hill of the Fairies, as "the little
folk" are supposed to have haunted it in bygone days.
Coming along from the direction of the bridge is Mr.
Stiven, shoemaker. At a glance it can be seen that he
is a man who must have endured great physical suffering, and to all appearance must have been a martyr to
rheumatism or some spinal affection. With a heroism
which is sometimes apt to be overlooked, he continues
his vocation with all the vigour left at his command,
and is thus able to earn a comparatively comfortable
living for a man in his position. These two young men
you see along with him are his twin sons, Donald and
William. The latter is serving his time in the *Herald*
Office as a compositor, while Donald has just received
an appointment as tutor on board one of Her Majesty's
ships of war. In connection with this family it may
be of interest to you to know that they are direct
descendants of one of Cromwell's Ironsides, who settled

in Inverness in 1657, and it is no flattery to say that, after a lapse of well nigh two hundred years, they still maintain the prestige of their ancestry. On the right hand side is the shop of Mr. Francis Wilson, who is busily engaged behind his counter serving several customers from Abriachan. As he is busy we will not interrupt him this afternoon. Just beyond Mr. Wilson's shop is King's Lane, the denizens of which are all of the working class. Further along, standing in his doorway, is Mr. David Birrell, tailor, who has a numerous family growing up around him. In consequence of an accident sustained in his youth, he is compelled to use a crutch, which he fondly calls his "pony." He is a most intelligent man, and is considered an excellent workman, being particularly good at the Highland garb and tartan work generally. He has in his time done work for many of the nobility of the country. Yonder tall gentlemanly-looking man is Mr. Campbell, shoemaker. By his side, amusing themselves, are his two little daughters—pretty lassies. Standing at the close-head is Mr. Thomas Fraser, weaver, familiarly known as "Thomas Tigh-chinn." He is conversing with his neighbour, Mr. Dyer, who, along with his two sons, has just returned after having finished the day's work at Holm Mills. What unearthly noise is that in the distance? It sounds as if some sea monster has got stranded and is gasping for breath. Oh! I see now what's the matter; it is one of Sandy Macrae's ("Ali Potheen") horses on the way home after the day's work. There is Ali himself driving. Let us have a word with him. "Your horse does not seem to be sound in wind, Sandy?" "No, 'deed, the brute, but the nuxt horse A'll get 'll no' be a 'roarer,' A'm tellin' you, though A wud pey five shullings for ut." We do not envy the fate of the poor

animal that will come Sandy's way even at a crown.
Even the tender mercies of the horse slaughterers at
the tannery are preferable.   We have now got as far as
the head of Fairfield Lane.   You ask me who that
dignified-looking, grey-bearded old man who has just
come along the lane is.   That is Mr. Macgregor, and as
you can see at a glance by his fine military, I might
almost say heroic, mien, he is one of that now fast-
diminishing band of heroes who fought in the Peninsular
War.   He was wounded in one of the early battles of the
campaign, and, to his great regret, became unfit for
further service, and was consequently invalided home,
where he has since remained, his fine soldierly bearing
being a subject of general comment.   Mr. Macgregor is
of a religious turn of mind, and even in his soldiering
days was looked up to by his comrades as one who
served his God as well as his King.   At the door of his
tavern stands another old soldier, David Fraser, who, in
addition to attending to his business here, is also
custodian of the Northern Meeting Rooms.   Next door
is the shop of Mr. Mackenzie, stoneware merchant, who
is a splendid specimen of his clan.   As you will observe
from that bill in the window, Mr. Mackenzie does not
confine himself to stoneware, but also deals in train oil,
which he sells in small quantities to the housewives in
the neighbourhood to replenish their cruses (lamps).
Mr. Mackenzie has charge of the pump there, which is
known as the East Pump, and he charges each family
who uses it the nominal charge of one shilling per annum
towards its upkeep.   That lady wearing green spectacles
who has just emerged from the doorway a little farther
along is Miss Miller, who keeps an infant school.   She
is popular with the children, having a wonderful way
with her.   That handsome, well-dressed man, who just
wished us "good evening," is Mr. Dickson, nursery-

man, whose nursery is in the neighbourhood. Just coming out of the door of his home there is Mr. Lachlan Mackintosh, barber, Church Street, who is just returning to his shop. That young man who has met him and is talking to him is his son Hugh. Mr. Mackintosh is a great reader of theological works, and as a result of his study has long since come to the conclusion that the Confession of Faith is wrongly named, and ought more appropriately to be called the "Confusion of Faith." In conversation with Mr. Mackintosh on religious matters he firmly impresses one that he is no believer in the so-called doctrine of election or predestination. Next door to Mr. Mackintosh is the residence of Mr. and Mrs. Macdonald. There they are coming along. They came from Glen-Urquhart some years ago, where they were familiarly known as the king and queen of the smugglers. In their day the worthy couple had many strange and stirring adventures with the gaugers, and usually had the best of it. That building with the thatched roof is the workshop of Messrs. Macdonald Brothers, cartwrights. On the street in front are two newly finished carts. That group of women you see there are standing around the West Pump. They are evidently discussing some momentous question quite out of the ordinary vein of daily gossip. Ah! I understand what they are now at; they are conspiring not to pay the usual shilling of water rate until the pump is put into a better state of repair. There is Mr. Cameron, the plasterer, conversing with Mr. Campbell, the gardener, the subject of their conversation being the excellent crops of the past season. As we are now at the end of Tomnahurich Street, and as it is too late to go as far as "Button Street" or the "Three Merry Boys," we will retrace our steps. On the opposite side of the street is

Mr. Duncan Mackintosh, weaver, who is, by the aid of
the setting sun, examining the web of wincey which he
has just finished. " Good evening, Mr. Mackintosh;
I hope you will find your job all right." " Oh, yes, it's
fairly good; I am very careful, and always try my best
to make a good job." What peculiar-looking, under-
sized man is that coming along, clad in short jacket and
wearing a broad Kilmarnock bonnet, while his breast
glitters with medals? Oh! I ought to have known him;
that is " Ali Beag na Creag" (Little Sandy of the Crag),
whose home is at Dunain. He has, as his decorations
indicate, been through several campaigns, including the
Peninsular. He was a drummer in the corps to which
he belonged, and although a small man, he was quite as
able to make a noise in the world as a much bigger one.
Here comes Macgillivray the sawyer ("Fire in the
Mountains"). He is easily known by his lame step.
He is accompanied by his fellow-sawyer (the topman),
Donald Macpherson ("Balchearlach"). They are
evidently in very deep conversation. Just as I
thought; Macpherson is strongly urging Macgillivray
to ask for more wages. "No," passionately exclaims
Macgillivray; "the less money I have I'm the better
off, because I have less to drink." That low-sized,
quiet-looking man who has just passed is Hugh
Macbean, tailor. He is a most industrious and unas-
suming man. We have now reached the tavern of
Mr. Martin. This gentleman has a promising family,
and is much respected in the neighbourhood. We
have now reached Young Street, at which point we will
part this evening. In our next walk we will deal with
this street, and also with the " Little Green," in which
latter place I hope to be able, among other things of
interest, to let you see how the Inverness people bleach
their clothes.

NOTE.—A good story is told regarding Mr. David Birrell, tailor, who is referred to above. As stated, he was in the habit of calling his crutch by another name. On one occasion he was getting it repaired by a tradesman in the Haugh, and not being able to go for it himself, he sent a small boy. The lad's instructions were to go for the "pony." Imagining that he was to ride triumphantly home on a prancing steed, the lad cut a switch on his way up. His surprise and disgust may be imagined when a crutch was presented to him.

The elder Mr. Dyer, whom we have referred to in the foregoing, was employed with his two sons at Holm Mills, they being weavers. He subsequently left Inverness to go to Canada, but the ship in which he sailed was never heard of after leaving this country. His two sons thereafter sailed for Canada, and are still alive and prosperous in the land of their adoption. Mr. Lachlan Mackintosh, the "Barber," as he was formerly known by, was a native of the quiet town of Fortrose, and for many years attended to the tonsorial wants of his many customers in the small shop in Church Street, opposite the Hunt Hall. On the invitation of his eldest son, Dr. Mackintosh of Hamilton, Ontario, Mr. Mackintosh, along with his wife and family, left Inverness for that city in 1854, where, assisted by his son Hugh, he resumed business, and lived well into the century.

CHAPTER XXIII.

YOUNG STREET—BRIDGE END—NESS WALK—
LITTLE GREEN.

IN our walk this afternoon we will get somewhat off the beaten track ere we part, and visit the Little Green, as I promised you the other day. Meantime we will as we step along take note, as usual, of anything of interest that may come under our observation. This is the spot (the junction of Young Street and Tomnahurich Street) where we finished off our last stroll. On the right hand side is Mr. Phemister's place of business. This gentleman, in addition to keeping a small grocery, is also the owner of an unpretentious candle factory. Oh, there he is coming out of the shop door. I will speak to him. "Good afternoon, Mr. Phemister; you will soon be getting busy at the candle-making now that the nights are getting long." "Oh, yes, for the poor people can't do without light. I would ask you round to see the place, only the tallow is undergoing the boiling process just now, and the odour is not quite agreeable to those who are unaccustomed to it." "We will call along some other time, then, Mr. Phemister, when we will be glad to have a look through the place. Good afternoon." On the other side is Mr. Duncan Fraser, meal dealer, conversing with Mr. William Macbean, baker, afterwards a bailie of the burgh. Let us go and get a snuff from Duncan. I see he has the box in his hand. "How are you, gentlemen?" "Let us have a sneeshan, Mr. Fraser." "Certainly; here you are,

take a pinch, and welcome." (Takes the snuff.) "Atchoo! atchoo! atchoo! That's strong Taddy you snuff."
"Oh, it's not that very strong; it's you that's no accus-
tomed to snuffing. You would think it queer, lads, to
know where I learned to snuff first. Well, it was in the
jail." "Oh, you were never in jail, were you, Mr.
Fraser?" "Indeed I was, and the cause of it all was
that when I was staying on the croft out at Kirkhill I
had a 'pukley' barley over one year, and I thought I
would make a drop of whisky for the New Year, but the
gauger came round, and it wouldn't do." "Well, well,
Mr. Fraser, such things will take place. We will now
be stepping along." That jovial-looking man going
into that public - house on the right is John Forbes
("Darling Jock"). His place is a popular resort of
country people, and particularly of residents of the
Caiplich. It is a favourite shop for wedding parties,
but I don't think there is one there now, for if there
were we would soon know by the hooching. That somewhat pretentious building, with steps leading up to it,
and almost facing the bridge (now the Glenalbyn Hotel)
is the residence of the Rev. Dr. Rose, second minister of
Inverness. Talking of Dr. Rose, does it not seem strange
that the degree of D.D. should have been conferred upon
him and not upon Rev. Mr. Clark, who has been so long
first minister of the parish? Of Dr. Rose I shall perhaps have something to say to you on another occasion.
Right across the street is the shop of Mr. Duncan
Rose, grocer. This gentleman is always very gracious
with his customers, and the result is that he is exceedingly popular and does a good trade. In shirt
sleeves, with his leather apron wrapped around him,
stands William Macdonald ("William Ruadh"), the
cobbler, at the close-mouth. He is as usual taking his
afternoon smoke, while he converses with Mrs. Fraser

("Jenny Voonie"). They are on the Church question.
William bitterly regrets the defection of the people from
the Church of his fathers. In speaking of the Free
Church, a favourite saying of his is, "It is not the Free
Church at all; it is the dear Church." Jenny Voonie
has now left William, and is going across to the river
for a bucket of water. Let us wander slowly up the
riverside. What crowd is that in front of Ness House,
the residence of banker John Mackenzie? Oh, I see;
this is the day of the marriage of Miss Mackenzie, the
banker's beautiful daughter, to Captain Grogan. Here
they come. In that carriage, drawn by a pair of
beautiful greys, are the newly-wedded pair, and as they
drive past, list to the huzzas of the bystanders. Look,
there is something interesting going on inside the gate
on the lawn. Mr. Mackenzie has brought all the guests
out, and to the music of that excellent reel and strath-
spey band, supplied by Mr. Lowe, they "trip the light
fantastic toe," with their host in the middle of them
enjoying himself to his heart's content. It would, I
think, be very difficult to imagine a more charming
picture than that now presented to us. Having spent
some little time at this point, we will now pass on. I
wonder who that distinguished-looking gentleman strolling leisurely along in front of us is. Ah, here comes
Sandy M'Lennan ("Skye"); he will tell us. "Who is
that professional-looking gentleman, Sandy?" "Don't
you know who that is? Well, that's Mr. Calvert, the
well-known teacher of elocution from Aberdeen. He is
engaged teaching the young people of several families in
town, including those of Mr. Carruthers and ex-Provost
Ferguson. I have often heard him repeat dramatic
pieces to himself as he passed along the street. Step up
gently and you will, I daresay, hear him at some Shakes-
pearian quotation just now." "All right, Sandy." We

will now get closer to Mr. Calvert. Sandy is right; there is the elocutionist, in rich, musical voice, reciting a favourite quotation from " Hamlet." Listen—

"What a piece of work is a man !
How noble in reason !
How infinite in faculty !
In form and moving, how express
And admirable ! in action, how like an angel !
In apprehension, how like a god !"

To our right is the high wall of Ness House grounds. We have now arrived at the Little Green, where there is quite an animated scene. It is washing day in town, and the servant girls have come from all corners of the burgh, as Portia's suitors did from all parts of the globe. In the sparkling, rippling waters of the Ness the army of maidens, assisted by laundresses of the Green, are rinzing or "syning" the clothes, while others are engaged fixing up the ropes. Now the operations in the river have been finished, and the majority of the women have begun to hang up the clothes, while others are spreading some on the grass for the purpose of getting thoroughly bleached. Why, can't you feel the fresh odour of the linen ? Already there is a magnificent display of linen, white as the driven snow, and the maidens can now afford time to have a chat while they gaze admiringly at their labours. The Green and all the clothes thereon is now entrusted to Mrs. Maclean (" Bean a' Mhuilleir "), whose duty it is to patrol the Green during the night, the result being that there is never any complaint. See, the maidens are now beginning to take their departure in groups, with their baskets under their arms. On the morrow they will return for the dry clothes, when the scene will be quite as lively as to-day. We will step further west. That benevolent-looking gentleman who has just driven past is Mr. Macgillivray of Dumnaglass, chief of the Macgillivrays, taking his afternoon airing. He has just made the driver stop, and he is bestowing alms on that poor woman coming along. This gentleman coming towards us is Mr. Baillie of Dunain, who is accompanied by his personal attendant, Mr. Deans, who just came north a few years ago to act as Mr. Baillie's valet. Perhaps you do not know that Mr. Deans is another Waterloo hero. The "Iron Duke," on that memorable day which settled Bonaparte's fate, with his usual forethought, ordered a strong detachment to be posted in the rear to keep the retreat open, and Mr. Deans was there with his battery of artillery, and consequently escaped the brunt of the fighting. We are now beneath the shade of the elm trees near the Infirmary. There is Miss Mackenzie, the matron, coming into town. Mr. Fraser, who leases the garden, stands at the door. Just coming out of the front gate there is Lord Saltoun, who stays west at Ness Castle, while accompanying him are Prince Wilhelm of the Netherlands and Dr. Nicol, one of the visiting doctors. Prince Wilhelm has just been shown over the building, and is just remarking that it is more like a royal palace than a hospital. Inside the grounds there is the general handyman, Sandy Dallas, who, with a broad grin, which some people call a smile, o'erspreading his visage, seems thoroughly pleased that the visitors found everything in such order. We will this evening retrace our steps, and will meet again at the end of Ballifeary Lane, when we will stroll out into the suburbs.

NOTE.—We may here observe that when Sir Alexander Matheson of Ardross became proprietor of the lands adjacent to Ness Walk he offered the Town-Council a piece of ground, together with a supply of water on Planefield Road, in exchange for the public bleachfield known as the Little Green. The offer having been

considered satisfactory was accepted. Plans were prepared, and the handsome row of dwelling-houses on
Ardross Street were erected. Subsequently St. Andrew's
Cathedral of the Scottish Episcopal Church was built at
a cost of £22,000. In the meantime Ness House, which
was occupied by the Royal Engineers, who were engaged
in making a survey of the north of Scotland, also became
the property of Mr. Matheson. On the completion of
their lease the house was demolished. Ness Walk was
considerably widened, and the handsome buildings occupying the southern side of Young Street and the
corner of Ness Walk, along with the Alexandra and
Palace Hotels and the stately residential mansions
known as Ardross Terrace, were then erected. Possessing a fine southerly exposure and looking up the valley
of the Ness, with the lovely hills of the Leys in the
background, the situation and view therefrom is all that
could be desired. The buildings are worthy of the beautiful situation they occupy, and together form the finest
residential property in town. It may not be generally
known that the eminent actor, the late Mr. Henry
Talbot (his proper name being Michael Calvert), was a
son of Mr. Calvert, to whom we have referred. Mr.
Talbot made his first professional visit to Inverness
twenty-five years ago, and was cordially received by
several of his father's former pupils who were then
resident in town. Perhaps one of the best known,
most useful, and most respected of our city fathers
was Dr. John Inglis Nicol. Having in view the
interests of the industrial classes in town, he early in
the last century set on foot the woollen manufactory at
Holm, which has for years proved such a boon in
providing employment for those who were willing to
work, and still continues to do so. Another example
of his forethought was his getting the Town-Council to

erect the substantial retaining wall at the foot of the Castle Hill at Ness Bank, which so effectually saved the hill from being undermined by the waters of the great flood in 1849. Dr. Nicol served several years in the Council, and attained to the civic chair. While unremittingly attending the patients who were smitten with the cholera during the epidemic in 1849, he himself succumbed to the fell disease, and was deeply lamented by all classes. A handsome portrait of Provost Nicol fittingly adorns the Town Hall.

CHAPTER XXIV.

NESS WALK (*continued*)—BALLIFEARY LANE—TOMNA-
HURICH BRIDGE.

WE decided, I think, when we had our last stroll to
commence our explorations this afternoon at the foot of
Ballifeary Lane, and we will accordingly walk leisurely
westward along the riverside until we arrive at that
point. Ah, here behind us comes Dola Young, flagon
in hand. He is on his usual errand to the Infirmary
for "broth." Dola was some time ago a patient at the
Infirmary, having lost several fingers at Anderson's
sawmill on Shore Street. While in the institution he
was so popular with the servants, that on leaving they
extended to him the privilege of receiving daily a supply
of broth or soup for home use. He is, as you will
observe, bare-footed, and the elasticity of his step
reminds us of the "ship of the desert." He is gaining
ground upon us, and will soon be up alongside us. I
will enter into conversation with him, but I had better
first give him a pipeful of tobacco. "Well, Dola, you
are on your way to the big house?" "Yes, going to
the 'Firmary for broth." "Oh, by-the-by, Dola, what
did you say when you got your fingers hurt?" "Tut!
tut! stop 'e engine; all 'e men i' mill tilled." (Tut!
tut! stop the engine; all the men in the mill killed.)
"Were you tired, Dola, the day that Adams was hung,
when you carried the 'maister' down to the Longman
on your back?" "Yus." "What did you see that
day?" "Saw lot o' people, man in middle, high up

'tween two sticks—fall—rope round neck—kick—then stop." "That was terrible, Dola, but how did you feel coming - back ?" "Awful tired, awful tired." "You will be going in here ?" "Yes; get broth." "Well, good day, Dola" "Day." Poor Dola is, as I told you when we came across him down at Waterloo Place some time ago, a harmless fellow, and a great favourite among both young and old, who, because of his simplicity, treat him with sympathy and consideration. These two distinguished-looking gentlemen, magnificently clad in the Highland garb, coming towards us are no less personages than John Sobieski Stuart and his younger brother. They are both officers in the Austrian army, and are under the impression that they are · grandsons of Prince Charlie. They have for some time been the guests of Lord Lovat at Eilan-Aigas, and are very frequently in town. They have a great fancy for everything Highland, knowing of the undying devotion to the cause of their reputed grandsire. So far as outward appearance is concerned, they certainly look quite regal, and clad as they are in the garb of our ancestors, they certainly remind us of the Pretender as he appears to us in the paintings which have come down to us, although possibly more swarthy looking. We are now at the foot of Ballifeary Lane, and, looking down the Ness, one cannot but be struck with the surpassing beauty of the scene as the crystal water shimmers and dances in the autumnal sunshine, and the trees in their variegated beauty remind us of the fall of the year, while in the background rises the Castle Hill and the old Steeple. "Oh, good afternoon, Bailie Simpson." "Good afternoon; better weather, isn't it?" That gentleman to whom I have just spoken is Bailie Simpson, retired merchant, and the proprietor of Springfield, that magnificent villa to the right hand side.

These two handsome lads accompanying him are his two
sons, John and James, who have been away at school,
and are home on vacation. The former is about to
study medicine, while James is intended for the Indian
army. That stately-looking lady walking on the lawn is
Mrs. Simpson, who is a daughter of ex-Bailie Lyon. The
two pretty little girls along with her are the daughters,
the Misses Florence and Elizabeth. The next house
is Ballifeary, which is occupied by Mr. Patrick Grant,
Sheriff-Clerk of Inverness-shire. Here is Mr. Grant,
who has just arrived from the Castle in his carriage.
That lady who accompanies him is Mrs. Grant, who, if
I mistake not, is one of that influential local family,
the Baillies of Leys. Judging from the slowness of
Mr. Grant's progress up the avenue, he is evidently
suffering from some affection of the limbs. We are
now at the newly-erected mansion of Eileanach, which
is occupied by Dr. John Mackenzie, younger brother
of Sir Francis Mackenzie of Gairloch. He has recently
returned from military service in South Africa, and
now acts as factor of the Gairloch estates for his
brother, Sir Francis. Mrs. Mackenzie is a sister of
Mr. John Inglis, a rising Edinburgh advocate. Here
comes the doctor himself in deep conversation with
his minister, the Rev. Joseph Thorburn, who was
recently elected minister of the first Free Church in
Inverness. Dr. Mackenzie is one of his elders, and
takes an unabated interest in forwarding the cause of
the new Free Church of Scotland. The doctor always
appears in the Highland dress (Mackenzie tartan) just
as you see him, and few, you will admit, suit it better,
not even the Austro-Celts of Eilean-Aigas. The two
fine lads who have just past us going into town are Dr.
Mackenzie's two sons, who have already chosen the
profession of arms, while inside the grounds are several

K

of the daughters of the family engaged at a favourite
outdoor game. We will not proceed as far as the
Islands to-day, so we will now retrace our steps for a
short distance and then proceed up by the lane towards
Ballifeary Farm. It seems a pity that this thoroughfare is so narrow, as it is most awkward for vehicular
traffic. This will, however, possibly be put right in the
course of time. We have got as far as the farm now,
and will step in, and get a drink of milk from Mrs.
Fraser, who is a kindly lady. "Good evening, Mrs.
Fraser. We have just been having a walk, and thought
we would call for a glass of milk." "Come away lads,
we are glad to see you. What grand weather we are
having! Just step into the little sitting-room here and
rest awhile." "Yes, that is real good milk, and so
refreshing. A plentiful harvest, Mrs. Fraser?" "Yes,
indeed, and nearly all safely in, and I am pleased to
say that there will be plenty of straw for the winter's
fodder and bedding." "We will now be going, Mrs.
Fraser. Good day, and many thanks." "Good day,
and 'heesht' you back." There is the old gentleman, Mr.
Fraser, in the stackyard thatching the stacks, while assisting him are his two sons, Huntly and Davie. There
are the two elder girls, Maggie and Mary, feeding the
poultry, while the two younger, Bella and Emily, are
seated outside studying their home lessons. The freshness
and simplicity of this ideal rural scene, and its close proximity to one of the busy haunts of men, recalls to my mind
the lines of Pope—"God made the country, but man made
the town." I should not at all be surprised if in the distant future this locality will be studded with residences,
and a very pretty suburb it would make, I am sure. To
the left is the lodge leading to Bught House, the residence
of Mr. Duncan Grant, advocate, but as that ticket
nailed to the tree says "Trespassers will be prosecuted,"

we had better not in the meantime attempt to explore the grounds. We will now go up as far as Button Street or "The Three Merry Boys," which is a small inn situated close to the bridge over the Canal at Tomna-hurich. There are Mr. Lyon and his daughter standing at the door of their dwelling, and further on is Mr. Grant, who is lifting potatoes in his garden, assisted by some of his family. At the door of the public-house are a group of Glen-Urquhart and Abriachan crofters, who are just after having "deoch an doruis," while one, more considerate than the others, has been giving his horse a bite of corn. There is Mr. Hossack, the bridge-man, opening the bridge, and we will wait to see the steamer pass. It is the "Edinburgh Castle," and our old friend, Captain Turner, is on the paddle-box. "You have a nice house here, Mr. Hossack?" "Oh, very nice, but I'm more concerned about my boat just now, for a lot of rascals of Tomnahurich Street boys stole it and took it up the Canal, and it may be swamped with the steamer now for all I know." "I hope not, Mr. Hossack. These boys are very provoking, certainly." As we have a long walk before us in order to get back to town, we had better return. We have yet to go through the Little Green, and then we will be finished with this side of the river. We will, accordingly, meet next time at the lower end of the row of elm trees, or "The Lav-enders," as they are better known.

NOTE.—It may be of interest to our readers to know that Mr. William Simpson of Springfield subsequently attained to the Provostship of the town, and in August 1847 had the honour of accompanying the late Prince Consort when His Royal Highness paid a visit to Inver-ness. He also attended the Northern Meeting Ball in the evening. Dr. Mackenzie of Eileanach also attained to the civic chair, and during his term of office was the means of doing much good work in the interests of the town. As Provost he had the honour of receiving Her late Majesty Queen Victoria on her arrival at the station after passing through the town. In her "Life in the Highlands" the Queen writes "that she was pleased to see the Provost of the town, a fine old gentleman in the Highland garb." The Queen's visit to Inverness took place in September 1873. The portraits of both Provosts adorn the Town Hall, that of Dr. Mackenzie being in the Highland garb. When Dr. Mackenzie sold Eileanach and built another mansion beside the Ladies' Walk the name Eileanach was given to the new residence. We may also mention that for nearly forty years the brothers known as John Sobieski Stuart and Charles Edward Stuart, to whom we referred, were frequent visitors to Inverness, and were known and cordially received by the neighbouring gentry. Residing first at Logie, on the banks of the Findhorn, they subsequently removed to a beautiful castle, built from designs of their own, on Eilean-Aigas, an island on the Beauly River, which was furnished in a sumptuous and tasteful manner. The brothers were strikingly handsome, were ardent sportsmen, cultured students and authors, but by what mysterious process they led themselves to believe that they were descendants of the royal Stuarts it is difficult to ascertain. It is evident, however, that they were deeply imbued with the spirit of Jacobitism and Scottish patriotism, and possibly an intense and protracted concentration of thought on this subject might have resulted in converting them to the belief that they really were what they professed to be. The elder brother died in February 1872, and the younger in June 1880. They are interred in a vault in the quiet churchyard at Eskadale, and a handsome Celtic cross of red freestone marks the spot.

Mrs. M'Kenzie of Eileanach's brother, Mr. John Ingles, won his first case at the Justiciary Court held at Inverness in 1832, was Dean of Faculty 1857, and was leading counsel at the trial of Madeline Smith, and subsequently attained the position of Lord President of the Court of Session as Lord Glencorse.

CHAPTER XXV.

THE LITTLE GREEN.

"This is the spot where we promised to meet," as the melodramatic hero says, beneath the ancient "Lavenders." The leaves are falling and the autumnal wind is whistling somewhat drearily through the almost denuded branches, reminding us that "gloomy winter" is drawing nigh; but, on the whole, the weather is seasonable, and we will, I hope, spend both a pleasant and a profitable afternoon in strolling through the neighbouring locality, which is one of the most interesting we have yet visited. We will at the outset direct our steps through "The Little Green." These two stately-looking gentlemen who have just passed are John Peter Grant, Esq., advocate, and Duncan Grant, Esq. of Bught. The former, who is laird of Rothiemurchus, is a frequent visitor to town, and during his visits is, as a rule, the guest of the Laird of Bught. See, they have just met Mr. Wardlaw Ramsay, who is coming into town. He is a well-known sporting gentleman, and one of the stewards of the Northern Meetings. What does this fire by the roadside and that huge pot standing close by mean? Ah! here comes our old friend, Mrs. Maclean ("Ben a' Mhulleir"); let us ask her. "What's up this afternoon, Mrs. Maclean?" "Ach, laadie, iss that ahl you know? This iss the nicht o' the big blanket washing, and the lassies wull be here with their baskets un a luttel, and the washing and the stramping will begin." "Oh, yes, Mrs., we understand what it is for now; indeed, we might have known. The fire seems to be blazing nicely." "Ach, yus, it's doing fine. Wan o' you laads micht gie me a lift on wi' the big pot, as it is too heavy for wan." "Certainly, Mrs. Maclean" (assists with pot). "Many thanks; it's very good o' you." "Not at all, Mrs. Maclean; good day." There, stepping out of her cottage, is Widow Fraser. On her arm she carries a large basket of clean linen for the Caledonian Hotel, for which establishment she is outdoor laundress. See, she has forgotten something; I can tell by the way she has suddenly come to a standstill, but as she considers it unlucky to return, she calls upon her devoted daughter, Katie, to come out to her. Look, there she comes with a small parcel, which she hands to her mother. Standing in the next door is big Rory Cameron, the shoemaker, taking the air. His florid, healthy-looking countenance is more like that of a man who lives in the open than one who is confined from morn till night. Here comes William Macgregor, the tailor, who works with William Fraser, clothier, High Street, "Good evening, William. How are you keeping, and how is the wife?" "The wife is just getting ready to help with the blanket washing." "Are you keeping busy yourself, William?" "Oh, yes, always busy. D'ye know a strange thing that happened over in oor shop thus week? We wuz making two coats for customers in Tain. The wan was green and the other black—I mean the coats,—and as we wuz working in a hurry to catch the north coach at four o'clock in the morning, as the coats wuz for a ball at night. What did we no do but put the green sleeves in the black coat and the black sleeves in the green coat. We got them back the day, and when we saw them we looked kind o' stupid, I can tell you, but it's a nesty thing working late at nicht anyway." "That was awkward, William, but mistakes will happen." "Oh, yes, indeed." A little bit further along is the cottage of Charlie Campbell, gardener. He is a jolly, blythe, good-hearted old fellow, and is a tolerable musician, his favourite instrument being the flute, which he used to play in the old militia band. Here he is coming along. "Good evening, Charlie; there'll be very little gardening doing this weather?" "Very little, but we're busy howkin' the tatties, and a good crop they are, especially the 'rocks' and the 'kidneys.'" In the attic above Charlie lives Miss Fraser, who is known among the bairns as "Nannie in the Garret." She is in feeble health, but manages to eke out a livelihood by "white seam." She is a great favourite with the children, who visit her room, and to whom she usually sings snatches of old songs. Listen! there is her voice—

> "I won't be a nun, I shan't be a nun,
> I'm too fond of pleasure to be a nun."

Although in feeble health, Annie has evidently no fancy for the "sacred" veil or the cloistered cell. We are now at the door of Miss Annie Macleod, who is a professional laundress, and who takes in pupils in the business. You know, laundry work is considered quite high-class, and it is thought no ordinary accomplishment to be a good laundress. Here comes Mrs. Fraser, the gardener's wife. She is, I have no doubt, looking for her two sons, Ali and Finlay. As the latter is always in some trouble or other, she is evidently anxious that they should both turn up. There they come tearing along, barefooted and bare-legged. Their mother has now got her eye on them. Hark! she is threatening them with a "plooching." "Oh, ye pair o' young vagabonds, wait till I get ye in the hoose.

Who d'ye think's going to be keeping your dennar warm for oors? There ye are efter wyding un the ruver agen, getting yur clothes weet and yer toes bludded. Ah, you micht hev sense, but you'll never hev sense." The boys have now vanished indoors, and as, mother-like, Mrs. Fraser's threats are worse than her blows, we may rest assured that their chastisement will be comparatively light. Coming up the lane is John Macleod, the clarionet player, who is one of the finest instrumentalists in town, having served his time in a crack regimental band. There is the old wife welcoming him at the door. The aged pair toddle lovingly down the hill of life together hand in hand. A few yards further on is the house of Duncan Macrae, another ex-military musician, whose instrument is the trombone, of which he is master. There he is, that tall man coming towards us, stepping along as if he were marching to the "Garb of Old Gaul," or some such martial air. Let us have a short "crack" with him. "You have just been over the town, Mr. Macrae?" "Yes, I was over having a look of the paper at Jimmy Macgillivray's; he gets it every week. There's not much doing, only the Irish are keeping things pretty lively; and, indeed, I am sorry to see that the wants of the crofters in the Highlands are not attended to as they should be by the Government, and the result is that hundreds of families are leaving for Canada and Australia, so the paper says." "That is so, Mr. Macrae, but let us hope for better land laws in our country." "Oh, I see your trombone hanging in the passage there; it is beautifully polished." "Of course it is; I take a pride in keeping it burnished, as every good musician ought to do." "Is that Sandy Chisholm, the shoemaker, hammering up-stairs?" "Oh, yes; Sandy's aye at it early and

late." "Well, good evening, Mr. Macrae, we'll not be
keeping you, as it is time you had your tea. We are
going to call on Cameron, the fiddler, down by." This
is the fiddler's door. Let us walk in. " Good afternoon, Mr. Cameron. How are you getting on now ? "
" Oh, fine." " Are things getting settled over at the
Chapel of Ease now ? " " Oh, yes ; we have got Mr.
Sutherland now, a grand preacher." "Have you heard
from your son Lachie, lately ? " " Oh, yes ; he is always
working at the tailoring in Christie's in Edinburgh."
" You like a tune of the fiddle still, Mr. Cameron ? "
" Of course ; it's the best instrument we have yet. I'll
take down the fiddle and give you a bit tune, ' The
Deil among the Tailors,' and indeed he's often enough
among them " (plays the air after much tuning of the
fiddle). " Thanks ; we'll now be going. Is this Christy
Jameson's house, Mr. Cameron ? " " Yes, and I think
Christy, poor old body, is in even now." Christy, as you
will find, is a most interesting old lady, her father being
once on the magisterial bench. Her style of dress is
quite antique. The thin, spare figure dressed in a
linsey-woolsey gown, with high " body," tight sleeves,
slightly puffed at the shoulders, and white muslin close-
fitting cap, over a face that would make a study for a
Raeburn or a Romney, reveals a maiden lady of the
real old school. We will visit her. (Knocks at the
door and then lifts the latch.) " May we come in, Miss
Jameson ? " " Come away and sit down." " Are they
all well with you ? " " They are wonderful, thank you."
" What are you busy at now ? " " Binding ladies' cloth
uppers for the shoemakers, and I am very thankful I
always get plenty of work." " You might give us each
a drink of your treacle ale, which is such a favourite
beverage hereabout. Is that the ' stooley,' lying in
the corner there, that you take to church with you on

Sabbath, Miss Jameson?" "Yes; I'm not able to pay for seat rent, so I just take it with me under my cloak and sit up beside the pulpit, where I trouble nobody." "You have never used it in the same way as Jenny Geddes, though?" "I would do that too if I thought there was reason for it." "We will now go, having partaken of your hospitality and enjoyed your crack, so good-bye just now, Miss Jameson." "Good night to you, and blessing be with you." We will now leave this locality, but will yet return to it, and continue our ramblings further down the lane. As we turn away from this humble locality, are you not strongly reminded of the lines of the poet Gray?

> " Let not ambition mock their useful toil,
>   Their homely joys and destiny obscure ;
> Nor grandeur hear with a disdainful smile
>   The short but simple annals of the poor."

NOTE.—It gives us no little pleasure to refer to John Peter Grant, Esq. of Rothiemurchus, as one of the most popular and outstanding gentlemen of his time. He was well known and his services were warmly appreciated by many in distress, and in whose aid he was always ready to yield his valuable assistance and advice. In those days when landlords were as a rule severe, and factors even more so, and when there was plenty of law and little justice, when crimes of little consequence were severely dealt with, Mr. Grant was sought for, and if he could be got to take the cause in hand, his client might feel satisfied that the case would be thoroughly investigated and every justice done. Mr. Grant was born in 1774 and died in 1848. His son, Sir John Peter Grant of Rothiemurchus, succeeded the notorious Eyre as Governor of Jamaica in 1866, in which capacity he rendered the country excellent service. We are very pleased to note that his grandson, of the same name, is with us now as the esteemed

representative of law and justice, and for whom we
desire to express every good wish.   Mr. Duncan Grant
of Bught, Writer to the Signet, was of a retiring disposition, and although his father filled the civic chair,
he himself, while taking a warm interest in local affairs,
never aspired to municipal honours.   By his will he left
£5000 to his native town to assist in building a new
Town House, expressly stipulating that access to all
meetings held in the audience hall should be entirely
free to townspeople.   Mr. Grant was born in 1801 and
died in 1873.   A memorial to Mr. Grant is shown on
the window above the principal entrance to the Town
House.   It consists of two panels in stained glass, containing fanciful portraits of Ossian and Sir Walter Scott,
as representing the ancient and modern poetry of Scotland.

CHAPTER XXVI.

TANNER'S LANE.

DESPITE the fact that this locality (Tanner's Lane) is a comparatively humble one, there is a fascination about it that makes us loth to leave it, so we will again this afternoon in the course of our "constitutional" visit that portion of it which we were unable to go through the other day. The weather is a little blustery, and the meteorological indications are not by any means reassuring, but we will button up our topcoats and face the elements cheerfully, for after all there is nothing half so bracing as a sharp autumnal breeze from the direction of the heather hills. We will possibly manage to finish our visitations on the north side of the river to-day, and now that we have arrived at the spot where we left off, we will lose no time in setting out, so that we may be able to finish our observations before darkness sets in. This elderly matron coming along is Mrs. Macdonald ("Peter's mother") with a pet jackdaw at her heels, following her like a dog. Let us speak to her. "How are you, Mrs. Macdonald?" "Oh, I canna complain, considering." "That's a very tame jackdaw." "Och, yes; poor jeckie. That's Peter's Johnnie Daw. It's a very funny beastie, and an awful thief. D'ye know it'll no leave a clothes pin or a spoon aboot the hoose, whatever it does wi' them. A'm afraid we'll hev to put it away." "When did you hear from your son Archie?" "Aboot a fortnight ago; he's always in the Indies in the seventy-eighth." "Is it true that 'Nannie

in the Garret' died this morning, Mrs. Macdonald?"
"Yes, poor cratur; but she was never strong, although
she had wonderful courage. The bairns will miss her
very much." "Hulloa! what dog is this?" "That's
'Dido,' poor fellow; . everybody knows him. He belonged to Willie Fraser at the Canal Bridge, and when
Willie died the dog made his home here, and sleeps on
Mrs. Macrae's mat inside the outer door at night. He's
a good-natured brute, and doesna bite the bairns. Poor
Dido" (pats him on the head). "Well, we'll be bidding
you good-bye, Mrs. Macdonald, just now, as we are going
down to have a look through the coach yard." "Good-
bye." This is the gate of the yard, and we will just step
inside. There is Mr. Campbell, the foreman, coming in
our direction. I shouldn't be at all surprised if he will
check us for trespassing, as he is pretty abrupt in his
manner when everything is not going smoothly, and he
looks pretty sulky to-day. We will, however, address
him in our most persuasive tones, and perhaps put him
in good humour. "Nice evening, Mr. Campbell. We've
just come to have a look round the premises, and we
hope you have no objection." "Imph! if you call this a
nice evening you are not particular. Don't you see that
ticket up there saying there's no admittance except on
business?" "We want to see Sandy Sutor, the painter,
for a few minutes, Mr. Campbell." "Very well, you can
come in if that's the case. There he is over there, but
be sure and don't hinder him from his work." "Thanks
very much." We will now go across to Sutor. "You're
busy, Sandy?" "How in the world did you manage to
pass Campbell, chaps?" "When we asked for you it
was all right. That seems to be a particular job you
are at, Sandy." "It is that, for its nothing less than
the royal coat-of-arms, as you see, that I am painting
on the panel of the Duke of Wellington mail coach,

and I can tell you it takes some work. Would you believe that I have to put five coats of the finest varnish over that, and when I'm done with it it will look like polished glass." "You are not so smart on foot, Sandy, as you are with your hands?" "No; I'm sorry to say I'm not." "How did you get the rheumatics, Sandy?" "I was working at a particular job down in Tain a number of years ago in a low, damp place, and I was so much taken up with my work that I got soaked through about the legs without noticing it. It seemed to take a hold of me though, and I never was the same since, but I must just be putting up with it. Talking about this puts me in mind of a man I met in with when I was in Tain. He was from Thurso, and got a summons to attend a Justiciary Court at Inverness; but not being able to pay the coach fare, he had to travel on foot, and being sound of limb, he could not get out of it. I went a bit on the way with him. He was a good man, and he told me many things that would happen me, and among others said that I would have great trouble with my family." "You have a large family, Sandy?" "Yes, but many of them died when quite young." "Oh, there's Frank Fraser, the blacksmith, coming out to weld the rim of a wheel." "You know him, d'ye? He's a rare old chap Frank, and, mind you, he's no' a bad fiddler: he often plays the bass to old Cameron up the lane. They tell me that Frank was a fine-looking fellow in his younger days, and that a young Inverness lady of aristocratic family once tried hard to get him to run away with her and get married, but he had too much sense to do any such thing. Look! there's Campbell's wife—'Big Flora'—giving him his afternoon lessons, and she'll not improve his temper, I can tell you. You'd better be shifting, for I can see he has his eye on us." "Well, we'll be going, Sandy. We don't want to get you into trouble." From the number of coaches which you observe lying about the yard it can be seen that a considerable amount of repairing work is done here, and the establishment is very appropriately called "The Coach Infirmary"; but I may mention by the way that the place was once used as a tannery, hence the name "Tanner's Lane." We had now better get outside, as I see Campbell making tracks for us, and it would be unpleasant to encounter him in his present mood. We are now again in the lane under the spreading branches of the elms overhanging the wall at the back of Banker Mackenzie's garden. There is Mr. Bremner, teacher, Raining's School, on his way to visit his father-in-law, Mr. Calder, meal dealer. We are now standing beside the door of Sergeant James Tallach, burgh officer. Here he is coming 'round the corner, on his way to his tea. "You're getting home, Sergeant Tallach? Man, that's a queer name you've got— 'Tallach.'" "That's not my name at all, although I'm called that. Mackenzie is my surname, and I belong to the Mackenzies of Kintail." "That's a pretty little girl of yours, sergeant?" "She is that, and she has a good right to be, for isn't myself and her mother good-looking, although it's myself that's saying it? She's just on her way from Miss Anderson's School on the Hill." "When had you word from your son Davie?" "He's just sailed along with his regiment— my own old corps, the 64th—for China the other day. I hope all will go well with him, poor fellow, in that strange land." "We hope so, Mr. Tallach." "I'll now be going in for my supper." "Well, well, we'll not be detaining you, and, in the words of Macbeth, 'May digestion wait on appetite, and health on both.'" This man coming along in his shirt sleeves, with leather apron tied round his waist, is William Ross ("Brocair"). He seems to be in haste. "Good evening, lads; I'm just going into Mr. Phemister's for half a pound of candles to finish a job in a hurry. Getting awfully cold, isn't it?" We will now go down as far as the head of Huntly Street to Sandy Fraser, the leather merchant's, which we visited already, as you remember. Just as I expected, the usual group of gossips are here—William Douhl, "Tailor Tasdan," "Danny from Raigmore," his father, and others. As the door is standing open, let us listen to their discussion. The subject under review is the days of their boyhood, and they are making comparisons of the long distances each had to travel to school. William Douhl claims that he had to walk five miles to school in the dead of winter, with a big peat under one arm and his books under the other. Listen! "Danny from Raigmore" is chiming in—"I hed to go farther than enny o' you." "When hed you to do that, Danny?" asks his father with surprise. "Ach I, long before you waz born, father." "Well, Danny, I'm done wi' you noo." That was rather a good one of Danny's, wasn't it? If we had only time to wait we would get more amusement at this shop door than at a Punch and Judy show, but as the night is lowering and the weather becoming more boisterous, we had better part. Next week we will meet at this spot, when, with your permission, I will have something to tell you of the stone bridge.

NOTE.—It may be of interest to state that at the time about which I write Miss Sutor, sister of my friend mentioned in the foregoing chapter, held the responsible position (at the Winter Palace, St. Petersburg) of head nurse to the Imperial family of the late

L

Emperor Nicholas, and nursed the present Emperor's grandfather and grand-uncles.

As we have now made the acquaintance of the trio of burgh officers—Sergeants Grant ("Supple"), Tallach, and Chisholm—and as they were for upwards of a third of the century very closely identified with the well-being of the burgh during that time, we feel a desire to linger longer with them. It is more than what is generally reckoned a generation since the custom of the town officers accompanying the Provost and Magistrates from the Town Hall to the High Church twice every Sunday of the year without intermission, the pomp and circumstance of the occasion being not wanting in interest. A few minutes before eleven o'clock the Magistrates and their escort, in full array of scarlet and blue plush and cocked hats and halberds, beautifully polished, the pageant formed up, and on the first stroke of the clock bell march off, and with a steady pace, keeping the middle of the street. The other bells have now stopped, but with deference to the city fathers the High Church bells continue ringing. On the arrival of the party at the west door two of the officers halt, face inwards, and bring their halberds with a steady movement to the order, while the left hand is raised to the hat by way of salute. Presently, Hugh Fraser ("Cromarty"), bellringer, assisted by John Macfarlane ("Morgan"), is careful that the last chap of the bell is executed just as their honours pass into the aisle, the halberds being carefully deposited in a receptacle behind the door. Meantime, "Supple," who is the senior officer, steps hurriedly before and opens the magisterial pew, and the party being now comfortably seated, takes their hats and walking sticks, and, quite after the manner born, carefully places them on pins behind the chairs, then he reverently takes his seat.

The Castle and Stone Bridge from Douglas Row.

The minister thereafter rises and gives out the Psalm, and the service is proceeded with. The same ceremony is observed at two o'clock in the afternoon, there being no service in the evening, for the reason that it was well on in the fifth decade before gas was introduced in the church. It was the custom up to an early part of the century for the Magistrates to return after service to the Town Hall, where they regaled themselves at the public expense, in the summer time with wine and cake, and in the winter with what was then known as mulled porter. The reason for this appears to us to be quite obvious; the sermon might be quite orthodox, but something withal to wash it down was evidently desirable. With the progress of the times such customs we have described do not now happily exist.

CHAPTER XXVII.

STONE BRIDGE—"TOM TIT'S" STORY.

THIS afternoon we will, as previously arranged, devote
our attention to the stone bridge, which has for many
generations withstood the ravages of time and the force
of wind and water, but which, I am afraid, will have to
go some day before the onward rush of the current if
the Ness rises much higher than it is at present.   Look
at that seething, roaring torrent, which is the natural
result of last week's heavy rains.   Isn't it marvellous
how the structure withstands its terrible force ?   As
the weather is particularly fine now, however, I would
suggest that instead of taking our customary walk we
linger for some little time in this most interesting
locality, and after I have told you something of the
bridge, we will direct our attention to some of the
passers-by.   This is market day, and the stream of
traffic, pedestrian and vehicular, which you see crossing shows what a necessity a bridge is to the commercial life of a community.   This bridge, which was
constructed in 1685, consists, as you will see, of seven
arches, the principal span being of course in the centre.
On the demolition of Cromwell's Fort at the Citadel
the stones were used for the erection of the bridge.   It
was built by a local contractor at a cost of £1300,
which seems a very small sum indeed ; but it must be
remembered that in these days one shilling was almost
equivalent to ten shillings to-day, the cost of labour
being almost nominal as a result of the remarkable

cheapness of the necessaries of life. The town arms, Macleod arms, and inscription were specially ordered from Leith. It took four years to build, and it may interest you to know that the date of its opening, which I have already mentioned, was a year or two before the Revolution, Charles II. being still on the throne. It was built by public subscription, the Highland lairds contributing handsomely, one of the principal sub-scribers being Macleod of Macleod. The town had considerable difficulty from time to time in raising assessments towards the upkeep of the bridge, and appointed as one of the town officers a master mason to see that the work of repair was properly attended to. It took the place of a wooden bridge that fell during an aquatic display on the river in the year 1664, there being about 100 persons on the frail erection when it collapsed. Fortunately, none of them were very seriously injured, although there was, of course, a wholesale immersion. In referring to the bridge on one occasion, one of Cromwell's officers said that it was "the frailest structure that ever straddled so wide a stream." It is recorded that there were several bridges over the river at this point, one being burnt by Donald of the Isles in the fifteenth century, during an incursion into the south. The town was without a bridge from 1664 to 1685. We will now step on to the stone bridge, but before we do so, I may mention that at this point—the end of Ness Walk—J. M. W. Turner, R.A., the great landscape painter, stood and sketched the scene for one of his paintings, an engraving of which serves as a frontispiece in one of the earlier editions of Sir Walter Scott's "Tales of a Grandfather." There is Hector Mackenzie, the tollkeeper, a grand old soldier, who was present with his regiment, the Ross-shire Buffs, at the Battle of Maida in 1809. Just look at the fine old fellow. He is still as regimental as a button-stick, and despite the fact that he has almost attained the allotted span, he would, I feel sure, yet be quite prepared to answer the old war-cry of "Tulloch Ard!" did his country need his aid. Let us have a short "crack" with the old veteran. "You are not so busy now, Mr. Mackenzie, as you used to be before you ceased lifting the halfpennies from foot passengers?" "No; not so busy. I only collect toll for the carriages now, and the petty customs, of course, and a wearisome job it is, I can tell you. If you could see how some of the people try to slip past when they think I'm off my guard in the toll-house, but I did too much 'sentry-go' in my time to let them pass without being challenged." "You have your work before you, we feel sure, Mr. Mackenzie; but commend us to an old soldier for the proper discharge of the duties of such a post as this." Does not the roadway seem inconveniently narrow for the traffic, and the parapet remarkably low? The cope-stones, which are of red freestone, are, as you will observe, pretty well secured, being clasped together by strong iron bands, and altogether the appearance of the structure denotes stability, although it is just possible that the foundations are gradually being undermined by the current. Ah! here comes the tall figure of Ali Watson, a well-known young fellow who is a bit "soft" in the head, and being very "biddable," is sometimes imposed on by young folk. On his shoulder he carries a bundle of cloth for our old friend, Mr. George Macleod, tailor, Huntly Street, who has just purchased it at Macculloch Brothers, so as to enable him to finish his Martinmas work. For the sum of 3d. he has engaged Ali to take it home. There is Mr. Macleod a few paces behind him, accompanied by Mrs. Chisholm. The pair of young "blades" who have just passed us and are now speaking to Ali are Jimmie Braid, the moulder, and Johnnie White, the ostler, a pair of regular wags. They have apparently just asked him to throw the parcel into the river, which he is in the act of doing, much to the consternation of Mr. Macleod, who has rushed forward in the nick of time and rescued the bundle from "a watery grave." White and Braid have passed on almost doubled up with laughter at the result of their practical joke. Oh, by-the-by, there is something here I wish specially to draw your attention to. Just take a look over the parapet on the right hand side and you will see a good-sized gooseberry bush growing on the outer ledge several feet down. You ask how it grew there. Well, the only way I can account for its appearance in such an unusual place is that dust from the road must have blown on to the projection and formed a kind of loam, while the rain and the spray from beneath, coupled with the fact that it had a southern exposure, gave to the small space a certain amount of fertility. Possibly, years ago, a bird dropped a seed there, or, indeed, it might have been blown there by the wind for aught I know, but in any case the result is the growth of the bush you now see, and possibly it will remain there as long as the bridge itself. Let us now step over to the opposite side and we will see another object of interest. Take a glimpse over there and you will observe above the buttress between the two arches an iron-stanchioned window. You will remember old John Maclean, the nonagenarian, having told us about the dungeon where "Donald Scholar" was confined. Well, that is the window of Donald's cell, the entrance to which was from the roadway here almost underfoot. The latter is now covered over with metal, but the apartment beneath still remains, and is doubtless the abode of rats. Could you imagine a more dismal place of confinement? The monotonous ripple of the water beneath, the weird moan of the wind against the window bars, and the rumbling noise of the overhead traffic, coupled with the gloom of the place, was surely worthy of the days of the Spanish Inquisition. Happily, the need for such dungeons has long since passed away. A little further along on the side of the bridge is the town arms, finely carved, while close by is the Macleod arms, and not far removed therefrom is an oblong stone measuring 7 feet by 3 feet, on which, you will observe, is cut in relief an elephant's hide. This forms a scroll whereon is inscribed the names of the Provost and Magistrates of the year 1681, and also of 1685. Why, we can read it upside down here—"Pontis Burgh de Inverness. Fundit 1681." Then follows, as you will see, the list of names, while the inscription ends with—"Finis 1685. Roberto Smith et Fils, archatecto, Forresino." Now, I think we have done quite enough in the way of bridge inspection. Let us therefore turn our attention to the "ever-moving throng" for a few moments. This conceited-looking little man coming along with an elaborate display of jewellery is no less a personage than Mr. Thomas Fraser ("Tom Tit"). Look out, he's got his eagle eye on us, and I can see his walking stick is already in position. (Mr. Fraser approaches and raises stick jocularly.) "Are you not afraid, lads?" "Well, we ought to be, Mr. Fraser, seeing that you are such a great warrior, fresh from the bloody fields of Spain." "Fighting for Queen Isabella is all right, but I would like to see my arrears of pay." "We were just looking at the bridge, Mr. Fraser. Can you give us any hints?" "Oh, yes, any amount. For instance, it was just up there a few yards that the Clan Fraser crossed the river on their way to Culloden." "How did the Frasers not cross the bridge?" "Well, you know, there was once a strong gate at the south end here, which I am told was held at the time by a strong party of the Argyle Militia, and as the Lovat clansmen did not think it expedient to attack the keepers of the bridge, they forded the river without waiting to dispute the passage. At the close of the decisive battle on the Moor the retreating clans fled down Bridge Street, and became congested at the south side of the gate, when Dr. Fraser of the Aird shouted, ' Good God, we must force our way, or we'll be all slaughtered. Don't you hear the Duke's bugles at the other end of the town ? ' The doctor led the charge, the gate was cleared, and the fugitive clans fled northward. Shortly afterwards Lord Kilmarnock was taken prisoner. During his flight he lost his headgear. At this point the old warrior's son, Lord Boyd, who was a Royalist officer, stepped up and placed his own hat on his worthy father's head, and turned regretfully away. Some say that this incident happened on Drummossie Moor, but I have good authority for saying it took place here." "Your conversation is most interesting, Mr. Fraser, but as it is getting dark, and as we have no time to stay, we will perhaps meet you at this point on the afternoon of this day week about three o'clock, when you will doubtless enlighten us further." "Certainly. Good night, lads." "Good night."

NOTE.—Jamie Braid, moulder at Wells' Foundry, and Johnnie White, ostler, to whom we have alluded, were well-known " lively " lads, who were expatriated by sentence of the Justiciary Court for the active part they took in connection with the Potato Riots, which took place in 1846. They never returned to Inverness again. The town's arms which were built in the masonry of the stone bridge were recovered after the flood of 1849, and built in the wall of the stairway of the old Town Hall. They are now to be found in the gable wall of the new Town House facing Castle Wynd. The Macleod arms, if we mistake not, are placed in the gable of Messrs. Mackintosh's wine shop, Bridge Street, a few feet from the pavement. The large slab on which is carved the scroll and inscription was also built into the upper stairway of the old Town Hall, and is now, we are informed, carefully deposited in a cellar below the Police Office! We desire in passing to pay our humble tribute to the nobility of character presented by that unfortunate nobleman to whom we have alluded, Lord Kilmarnock, who at his trial made such an excellent defence, and properly pleaded some consideration for the kindness with which he had always treated Royalist prisoners. So nobly did he speak that Lord Leicester said to the Duke of Newcastle, "I never heard so good an orator as Lord Kilmarnock; if I were you I would pardon him and make him Paymaster of the Forces." On his way to the scaffold Lord Kilmarnock embraced his companion in misfortune, Lord Balmerino, and said, "My lord, I wish I could suffer for both." It may be of interest to state that the present title of Lord Kilmarnock (now one of courtesy) is held by the eldest son of the Earl of Errol, High Constable of Scotland, who is married to a daughter of Sir Allan Mackenzie, Bart., of Glenmuick, and a great-granddaughter of the late Provost John Mackenzie, M.D., of Eileanach. In connection with our reference to the passage of the Clan Fraser across the Ness on their way to join the Highland army at Culloden, we may mention that in the early part of last century a shoe buckle of antique design was found in the bed of the river near the place alluded to.

Toward the end of January 1849 there was a heavy

fall of snow in the vicinity of the Great Glen of Scotland, followed by a sudden thaw; this had the immediate effect of raising the several rivers to an unusual extent, the Ness particularly so. I remember passing along the stone bridge on the afternoon of the 27th, the river was then very high and was evidently still rising, the authorities becoming alarmed for the safety of the bridge. The flood slowly but surely increased, and on the morning of the 29th the piers at the east end gave way, and in a short time the whole fabric yielded to the force of the stream. The gas pipe connecting the west side of the town with the gasworks being carried along the bridge, was broken, and for the later hours of the morning the town was in darkness. For more than a year the only means of passage, except the Black Bridge, was by a boat, the "Jenny Ness," certified to carry thirty passengers, the fare being one halfpenny. The pier was at the foot of Bank Lane, and during the winter "spats," it was no unusual occurrence for the boat to drift down as far as Wells Street. Subsequently a rather neat and substantial wooden bridge, adapted for foot passengers and hurleys, was set up on the Ness at the south end of Gordon Place, which proved a great convenience. In June 1852 operations began in connection with the erection of the present handsome Suspension Bridge, and after several futile attempts were made towards its erection and completion by several contractors, the unfinished bridge was subsequently taken over by the Board of Works, and great progress was made forthwith. The contract for the iron work, which has been so much admired, was successfully carried out by the late Mr. John Coats of Newcastle. This bridge was opened for traffic in August 1855, and cost £29,000.

CHAPTER XXVIII.

STONE BRIDGE (*continued*)—QUEEN MARY'S VISIT—
TOM TIT'S STORY (*continued*)—BRIDGE STREET.

WE are now at the east end of the stone bridge, and,
as you will remember, we made an appointment with
our old friend "Tom Tit" to meet him at this spot
this afternoon. We are a little before time, however,
and as it would be unfair to disappoint him, we will
linger about until he makes his appearance. As the
locality is an exceedingly interesting one, and the
weather exceptionally genial for this season of the year,
we will be amply repaid for the delay. You ask who
these three distinguished gentlemen are who have just
come down Bridge Street and turned west the riverside? They are, I may tell you, no less personages
than the recently-elected Provost, Dr. Nicol, Mr.
Andrew Smith, of the well-known and old-established
drapery business on High Street, which I already
pointed out to you, and Mr. Donald Fraser ("Donald
Soft"), of the cloth and linen warehouse, High Street.
The two latter gentlemen are accompanying the Provost
to his residence at Murray Place, and their talk is on
matters municipal. These buildings opposite, extending
southward towards the Castlehill wall, are known as
Gordon Place, which name has presumably been
derived from the Dukedom of Gordon, the family being
hereditary keepers of the Castle for centuries, and,

indeed, still retain the title. The houses are evidently
part of a number of buildings which clustered around
the Castle or fortress for protection from the sudden
incursion of an enemy in olden times. Similar groups of
buildings are also noticeable in other towns of importance, as, for instance, Edinburgh and Stirling. The
third house has been long occupied by Mr. Allan
Macdonald, cartwright, father of the gifted young
assistant of the High Church, the Rev. D. Macdonald.
The old gentleman is a famous maker of spinning
wheels. There is his sign—a wheel—above the doorway.
It may interest you to know that his son, who is likely
to rise in the ministry, was even in his boyish days not
only ahead of his school-fellows as a scholar, but also as
an athlete, and as a runner he beat the record, being
able to outstrip all others in the customary juvenile
race round the Castlehill. We will now have another
look at Castle Tolmie on the north side of Bridge
Street. Observe how closely it abuts to the end of the
bridge, leaving but a narrow passage leading down
towards Bank Street. Why, that message-boy with
his " hurley," as he rattles along, has nearly upset
poor " Ali Oulah " in the pathway. Let us now move
round towards the back of the Castle. You will
observe that it is the sixteenth century style of architecture, strong enough certainly, but with no great pre-
tentions to beauty of design. The windows, as you will
see, are most irregularly set, while the crow-step gables
add to its antique appearance. At the back of the
wine shop is the wretched ruin, said to have been
the residence of Mary Queen of Scots during her ten
days' stay in Inverness in 1562, which I think I
pointed out to you without much comment on a former
occasion. It is, as you can at a glance notice, very
unlike a sixteenth century edifice, much less a place

where the Queen would be received, but possibly further
light will be thrown on it in the future. It is
a pleasant reflection that such a high personage as
Mary Queen of Scots visited our town. She came in
rather depressing circumstances, but the loyalists
in the north soon flocked to her standard, and enabled her to assume her rightful place. In connection with her visit there is a charming little story
told, to the effect that a Ross-shire lady came across the
ferry and presented Her Majesty with thirteen stalwart sons, all dressed in Lincoln-green, fully armed,
and mounted on smart garrons, a bodyguard which
any monarch might be proud to accept. We will now
retrace our steps round by the front of the building.
Under the sign of "The Golden Last," in Castle
Tolmie, stands Mr. Gibson at the door of his establishment. He is a last-maker for the shoemaking trade in
town, and, indeed, for aught we know, he may prove to
be the LAST of his profession in our midst. To the
right of Bridge Street is the shop of Messrs. John
& James Fraser, painters. That man you see inside
with a profusion of red hair and an equally towsy
beard, which reminds one of "Dougal Cratur," is William
Shaw, one of the workmen, who is engaged mixing
paints, while young Donald Fraser is there by his side
lettering some packing-boxes for Donald Macdougall,
High Street, which are going abroad. I have already
described the remainder of Bridge Street to you, so that
it is quite unnecessary to again make reference to the
buildings and premises thereon as we step along. Well,
well, here comes "Tom Tit." We almost forgot about
him. "You are late, Mr. Fraser?" "I am indeed,
lads. I'm very sorry having kept you, but I was up at
the Post Office seeing if there was a letter for me with
my deferred pay, for I think it is about time I was

getting it now; but the Spanish Government is not much to be depended upon; it's not like our own." "That's right, Mr. Fraser; there's no Government to fight for like the home Government. But, by-the-by, talking about fighting, let us return to the '45 and the slaughter on Drummossie Moor. You would, I am sure, have known some in your younger days who were at the battle?" "Oh, yes, many. I remember one wife, Peggy Mackintosh, who stayed on Stephen's Brae, and when she was a young lass she went out to see the fight, the interest she had in it being that her brothers and her sweetheart were in the army of Prince Charlie." "Can you remember what she said about the battle, Mr. Fraser?" "Oh, yes. She described the two armies in combat being 'like a pickle peas dancing on a hot girdle,' and I never forgot her quaint and forcible description of it." "You had relatives yourself there, I think?" "Oh, yes; and you had relatives there too. Do you know, it was your father's granduncle, Donald Fraser, the blacksmith, that peppered the Earl of Loudon's night surprise army at Moy? Poor Donald! he had to run away to Stornoway, where he was forced to remain for three years away from his young wife and family." "The pity is, Mr. Fraser, that so many valuable lives were sacrificed for such a cause." "Oh, yes; but the clansmen had to do many a thing 'ta please ta laird.' Here we are, lads, at the jail door, and I have an invitation here to-night. This is the night of the prisoners' weekly dance." "How in the name of goodness do they manage to arrange a dance within prison walls?" "Oh, that's easily managed by keeping the jailor, Mr. Cameron, 'White Hattie' (called from his choice of head gear), in good humour. You see, there are a number of debtors in custody, and, of course, they get liberties, and the other prisoners are permitted to

join with them." "Oh, yes; we have always the
debtors with us, Mr. Fraser. There's a good deal of the
nature of the reiver about them. How do they manage
for refreshments?" "Very easily. The visitors take
a little each in with them, and then, when the drink is
exhausted, an empty bottle and also a small bag containing the money are lowered to messengers from the
public-house, just in the close at the back of the jail,
and I can assure you that it does not take very long to
replenish the supply. Napoleon would have called this
'adapting efforts to obstacles.' You see, they begin
kind of early to keep prison hours. I see John Beaton
looking across the street at me. He is a great T.T.,
and he thinks I am one too. If he sees me go in here
he'll be a little dubious. I see he has turned his
head, so I'll just slip in. Good-night, lads. I'm sorry
I cannot go further with you, for I meant to have a
long chat." "Tom Tit" is a wonderful old fellow, and
has had many varied experiences, and his reminiscences
are most interesting. He could tell of many strange
affairs in which he himself took part, but Culloden is a
favourite topic of his, and he made a hobby of gathering up as much information about it as possible. Talking of the Rebellion and Culloden reminds me of an
incident that took place on the afternoon of the battle
exactly at this spot (the top of Bridge Street). While
some of the rebel prisoners were being marched along
the street undue harshness was exercised towards them
by the Hanoverians. Several of the Scottish officers in
the royal army took exception to the manner in which
their countrymen were being treated, and were not
backward in expressing their disapprobation. Instantly
swords were drawn, and a melee ensued, which might
have had a very serious ending had it not been for the
interference of "the Butcher." The alarm was at once

given to the Duke, who was dining in the inn known as "The Horns," which was situated in the close where Mrs. Park's inn now is. Along with his henchman (the now notorious General Hawley, the vanquished of Falkirk) His Grace instantly appeared on the scene, and peace was restored. On learning the cause, Cumberland gave his assurance that the Scottish officers, who were always loyal to the crown, would not be further dealt with. Thus peacefully ended the dispute. We delayed too long in the vicinity of Castle Tolmie this afternoon, and we will therefore not have time to take in Church Street, which it was my intention to have done. It is altogether too interesting a street to get over hurriedly, so we will try and devote part of our next walk to it. We will now part. "Oidhche mhath dhuibh an drast."

NOTE.—Some time previous to the date about which we write, there took place a Revolution in Spain, when the Carlists attempted to deprive the Queen Regent, Isabella, of the sovereignty and place their own candidate, Don Carlos, on the throne. The Government being ill prepared to offer effective resistance, an appeal was made to friendly States for some form of assistance. Our Government granted the Queen permission to recruit men throughout the country, to be known, if we mistake not, as the British Contingent. An officer coming to Inverness for the purpose of recruiting, readily obtained about forty men of that class usually found in towns, and who are always "waiting for something to turn up." Our friend, Mr. Fraser ("Tom Tit"), was one of the warriors who volunteered; but before reaching the scene of operations the revolt was brought to a termination, and their services were not required. They were

M

consequently sent home without receiving any monetary acknowledgment of their enthusiasm. When our attention was called, nearly sixty years ago, to the site and ruin on the spot where it is said that Queen Mary resided during her ten days' residence in Inverness, it readily occurred to us that it was a very unlikely place, or even locality, for the most exalted lady in the land to take up her abode even for such a short time. It has lately been established almost beyond contradiction that there were dwelling-houses of a substantial character at the time of the Queen's visit on the south end of Bridge Street, at the foot of the Castle Hill, and overlooking the river. Provided the buildings on this spot, now known as Castle Tolmie, afforded the requisite accommodation, it would be a much more likely locality than that which has been pointed out as the Queen's lodgings. After the great flood in 1849, when the demolition of old Castle Tolmie became necessary, we recollect observing the difficulty experienced in the work of disintegration, the walls being of immense thickness, while the stones employed in the building were of small size, but the lime or cement used held the mass firmly together. The pointed stones on the roof windows had a variety of initials and emblems carved on them. These were subsequently removed to Redcastle and placed in conspicuous positions on an extension of that building. The gift of the Ross-shire lady to Queen Mary reminds us of an incident that took place during the visit of His Majesty, King George IV., to Edinburgh, in August 1823. At the levee, which was given at Holyrood Palace on this occasion, Sir George Sinclair, Bart., of Ulbster, presented his six daughters to the king, each being six feet in height. Just fancy thirty-six feet of daughters. The last survivor of the ladies was Miss Catherine Sinclair of Ulbster, who, for her many works of philanthropy among the humbler classes in the city of Edinburgh, won the warmest esteem and affection of the community. This lady died in 1864, and a handsome Gothic monument has been erected to her memory, by public subscription, in the west end portion of Queen Street Gardens, Edinburgh.

CHAPTER XXIX.

TOP OF BRIDGE STREET—THE STEEPLE—TOM TIT'S
STORY (*concluded*).

WE have met a little earlier than usual this afternoon,
and instead of going down Church Street, I think we
should linger for some little time at this very important
spot—the junction of High Street, Bridge Street, the
Castle Wynd, and Church Street—a spot which may
not inaptly be designated the hub or pivot of the town,
around which the community revolves. Here are to be
seen rich and poor, gentle and simple people in all the
varied walks of life, some clothed in broadcloth and
others in hodden grey, all bent on their own particular business. Take for example Donald Fraser
("Donald Iron"), who is just having a talk with
another member of the clan, Alexander Fraser, draper
("Skelpan Sanny"), while between the pair the snuff
mull is being vigorously assailed. Donald's garments,
as you will observe, are most fashionable, and the
buttons are of his own peculiar choosing, showing
clearly, as Polonius says, that the garment oft be-
speaks the man. He is indeed a veritable tailor's
model, and further, he is ambitious, so ambitious indeed
that it is said he even aspires to the civic chair, but as
to whether he will ever ascend to that elevated seat,
or even the magisterial bench, is a question which is
difficult to answer. If he does it would be well if
some modern Portia were close at hand to whisper
in his ear—

" The quality of mercy is not strained,
    It droppeth as the gentle rain from heaven.
    It is twice blessed, it blesseth him that gives and
        him that takes," &c.

That ferocious-looking animal at his heels, which, it
strikes me, we have come across before in our walk,
is his favourite bull-dog " Crib," " whose bark is worse
than his bite," but who is, nevertheless, like the rest of
his species, quite as hardy as he looks, and is acknow-
ledged to be the only dog in town that can make a fair
stand before Raigmore's " Lubo." Indeed, judging from
that fresh scar across his " Berkshire "-like nose, he
looks as if he had been engaged in combat quite recently. Those three gentlemen passing down Bridge
Street are the sons of the late Duncan Forbes of
Culloden, Arthur, Duncan, and Joseph, the latter being
smartly attired in the Highland garb, which gives him
quite the appearance of being a worthy scion of a
noble stock. Behind him, conversing with Arthur
Robertson, laird of Inshes, is their tutor, Mr. Macnab.
Both the latter gentlemen, as you can overhear, are
eagerly discussing the law of entail. Mr. Macnab is a
great Free Churchman, and although a layman, occasionally occupies the pulpit. Indeed, it may be said
that he it was who preached the first Free Church
sermon in Inverness. In that shop door at the corner
of the Wynd stands Mr. Robert Fraser, clothier, who
has begun to converse with two well-known lairds,
Abertarff and Culduthel, who are just about to enter.
Hullo! there goes Johnnie Thomson, Fraser the baker's
lad, going down to the prison with a basket of " baps "
on his head for the prisoners. " White Hattie," the
jailor, seems to be anxious, and is out on the pavement
waving the young man to hurry up. Looking at the
prisoners' scanty allowance, one is forced to wonder

whether these "loafies" will increase in size on the
passing of the Corn Laws. Just below Robert Fraser's
shop is the establishment of Mr. Maclennan, silk
mercer and haberdasher; while that smart young man at
the doorway arranging some goods is Mr. Robert Grant,
nephew of Provost Cumming. Right below the steeple is
the scavengers' depôt, for it is here that their besoms
and implements are stored. Talking about the steeple,
now, isn't it really a handsome spire? It was erected
in 1790 (the same year in which the prison was built).
The steeple was put up by public subscription, Bailie
Inglis of Kingsmills being the treasurer. This edifice and
the Northern Infirmary are two lasting monuments to the
public spiritedness of a noble Highland gentleman, in
whose veins, it is said, there flowed the blood of King
Robert the Bruce. Well, well, here comes "Tom Tit"
again. He never seems to be off the street, but most
old military men like to show off their figures a bit.
"How goes Mr. Fraser? I suppose you had a good
night at the Prisoners' Ball last week?" "Oh, well,
just middling. It was a little bit 'driech.' You see,
after all, that really a prison with its unhappy surroundings is a poor enough place for a merrymaking. You
are still prowling around, boys, gathering up bits of
information, old and new?" "Yes, Mr. Fraser. Have
you anything else to tell us?" "Oh, I could tell you
enough about this town and the people in it to fill a
book. I suppose you don't know that the Fish Market,
which is now held at 'The Butchery,' used to be held
down the street, close to the pavement in front of
the prison, and that the prisoners who were in the
corridor getting an airing were in the habit of throwing
over a line from the windows, to which those on the
street used to attach pieces of bread, and on the word
'haul up' being given, the scones were not long in dis-
appearing. Occasionally a fish used to be attached,

and sometimes a fishwife was hooked on by practical jokers, which caused a good deal of merriment as the usual cry of 'Mercy me; what's wrong?' proceeded from the woman, who felt that an attempt was being made to drag her into prison. I need not tell you that fishwives were too heavy for the line, which usually broke when they were attached. 'Supple,' eagle eyed, sharp of hearing, and fleet of limb, attracted by the commotion, would soon be on the scene, and in a moment quiet would be restored." "Wasn't the Black Hole beside the corridor just a few feet on the down side of the steeple, Mr. Fraser?" "No; it was over below the Town Hall, the present office of the Savings Bank." "I suppose the authorities used to be very severe on poor unfortunates in your young days?" "Yes; very severe indeed. They put me in mind of old Lord Macqueen of Braxfield, who used to say, 'Show me the man and I'll show him the law.' It was no uncommon thing to flog men and women by the hands of the hangman at the corners of the streets, although their offences were but trivial, and they were even sometimes tied to a cart and dragged through the town. The last I can recollect of being flogged in this way was 'Bargain Mannie.' Indeed, up till very lately the law, or rather the 'law-dealers,' were unduly harsh in Inverness. Just look what they did quite recently— what the Justiciary Court did to the three boys, including Tibbie Main's son, who appropriated a few coppers in the Seceders Church in the Black Vennel. They were banished to Botany Bay. Poor chappies, it may be for their good, but it was hardly intended for that." "Oh, by-the-by, Mr. Fraser, do you remember when the 'marches' were ridden round Inverness?" "No, I scarcely remember so far back as that, but I knew two men who, as lads, were whipped at Culduthel in order to remember the particular locality." "Why don't they ride the marches now?" "Oh, that is very easily answered; simply because there are no marches to ride, the Council having managed to dispose of the properties by dividing it among themselves and otherwise." "How did they manage to do that, Thomas?" "It was the simplest matter imaginable to give away what did not belong to them when there was no check on them." "The passing of the Reform Bill would have put a stop to that kind of thing?" "Oh, yes, as far as self-election is concerned, but the old habit of appropriating other people's property dies hard. Don't you know that in the days I speak of there were two classes in town, the free burgesses and the vassals, very much the same as the Roman patrician and plebeian. The burgesses of course, being the favoured class, were partial to one another, while the vassals were entirely at their mercy. Seventy-two hours a week was the order of the day for workmen, while the burgesses, who knew their Bible well, believed in literally making their servants 'earn their bread by the sweat of their brow.'" "Did these burgesses make money, then, Mr. Fraser?" "No, indeed; the majority of them scarcely made as much as would endow a tombstone, but tyranny seemed so gratify them. The great ambition of aspiring young men of the vassal class was to become burgesses, or even be permitted to marry the daughter of a burgess, the reason being that they in their own sphere were oppressed in every way and precluded from doing any work or business on their own account except by permission of the Guild of Burgesses, and if they violated this rule they were liable in £50, failing payment of which they were sent to prison for a lengthened period. These men were oppressors, but the Councils of the time were worse. The passing of the Reform Bill was the great charter of deliverance for the people, although, as I have hinted, there still lingers much of the old spirit till this day. The first step in the direction of freedom was the 'sacking' of the great local tragedian, 'The Hangman,' whose 'princely' emoluments meant something to the community." "If these were what they call 'the good old times' we have another name for them, Mr. Fraser. Hark! the old clock on the steeple overhead announces that it is time we were parting, as we have some other business to look after this evening. We have lingered so long listening to those interesting yarns of bygone customs in 'the Clach,' and your crack has been altogether so entertaining, that we will require to put off our walk down Church Street for another day. Look, there are the 'scaffies' putting past their besoms for the day, which is a hint that we too should be making tracks for home. Good night, Mr. Fraser, and thank you for your information."

NOTE.—By the exercise of considerable perseverance our friend Donald "Iron" did attain to the magisterial bench, where he invariably took the opportunity of displaying his intensely "hard" nature on the erring ones who had the great misfortune to be tried before "his honour." On one occasion a soldier on the recruiting service in town, being from home, arrived late at his lodgings, and, not being expected, had to make some little noise to arouse the landlady to give him admittance. One of the stupid old "Charlies," who were then employed as night watchmen, came on the scene, and had the poor fellow taken to the police office. Next morning he was placed in the dock before Bailie Fraser, and, without much ado, received the usual sentence of sixty days. The soldier's friends in town thought this sentence was too severe for a law-abiding citizen seeking admission to his lodgings, even at a late hour. The matter was reported to the War Office, and the

authorities there at once sent an official to investigate
the affair, the result being that the sentence was
instantly squashed. Meantime the bailie received an
intimation from the Home Office that his commission
as Justice of the Peace was duly cancelled. Donald
" Iron " had a smithy in which a deal of work was done,
situated at the top of Market Brae. He also did an
extensive business in the tinsmith trade, in the close
at the back of his shop in High Street. Altogether he
seemed a prosperous man, until a financial crisis came
which could hardly be averted, and forthwith the man
of iron and tin retired into obscurity — " Sic transit
gloria mundi." As we have already remarked, the town
steeple was erected by public subscription, and the
work carried on simultaneously with the new jail.
We have no recollection of hearing the names of the
architect or contractor of the works. Strange to say,
their names did not survive long in connection with the
buildings they erected. The spire is 150 feet in height,
being 50 feet less than Sir Walter Scott's Monument in
Edinburgh. As the result of the earthquake which
took place in Inverness in 1815, a considerable portion
of the spire was thrown off the perpendicular, and
remained in that condition for several years. The late
Hugh Miller in " My Schools and Schoolmasters " refers
to this fact, and remarks that in its oblique position it
was one of the greatest curiosities in Europe, equalling
the Leaning Tower of Pisa. The authorities, however,
wisely decided to get the damage repaired. The late
Mr. James Fraser, painter (" Jamie Lazy "), who in his
time was a most worthy townsman, undertook the work
of adjustment, having carefully put up a scaffolding,
and then dealt separately with each stone by putting it
into its proper place until the work was satisfactorily
completed. The letters on the clock dials have been
frequently re-gilded. About twenty-six years ago it

was found that the cement between the stones was beginning to crumble, and the structure was otherwise in an unsafe state. The work of repair was entrusted to a firm of steeplejacks who were at the time doing some work in town. They gave the steeple a very complete overhaul, and placed thereon a lightning conductor. The weather vane and large and small balls were taken down and re-gilded as a free gift by the late Bailie D. Macdonald, painter, Bridge Street. The weather vane is made of two sheets of copper, bent out at the sides and joined together with rivets—a very crude example of the coppersmith's art. The vane is about 35 inches long. To see the balls and vane replaced was a sight long to be remembered. There were placed in the large ball several coins, photographs, local newspapers, documents, and a pint bottle of Milburn whisky! With reference to the very stringent laws formerly in force under the old burghal *regime*, we desire to point out that men who served the King in the army or auxiliary forces could claim exemption from the penalties exacted by the Corporation when desiring to commence business on their own account. Mr. Robert Grant, to whom I have referred on page 182, was subsequently for many years closely associated with the well-known firm of MacDougal & Co., the Royal Tartan Warehouse. Mr. Grant was promoted one of the first volunteer officers in town, and for many years was the popular commanding officer of " B " Company, 1st V. B. Cameron Highlanders, and was among the first to be awarded the Victoria decoration for long service, and having attained the rank of colonel, retired from the service several years ago. Colonel Grant having declined active business, continues his usefulness as a county councillor and as one of His Majesty's Justices of the Peace for the county.

CHAPTER XXX.

CHURCH STREET.

As we have no appointment with "Tom Tit" this afternoon, we will possibly get over a very much larger
stretch of ground than we did at our last meeting. As
you will remember, our walk on that occasion, like a
certain Irishman's, consisted of one long "stand." The
northern blast blows snell and sharp, and the snow-
flakes are eddying and swirling around the old steeple,
while the slight covering of snow on the ground tells us
clearly that to keep the blood in circulation we had
better be moving on. So we will leave this spot (the
head of Bridge Street) behind, and jog down Church
Street, where there are many objects of interest which
are worthy of even more than a passing notice. At the
outset I may mention that the street was, even five
centuries ago, referred to in legal documents as La Kirk-
gate, being the road leading from the Market Place or
the Cross to the Church. In days long gone this
thoroughfare was doubtless the scene of many a gallant
pageant wherein lords and ladies gay took part. Methinks
that even now I can hear the clank of the scabbard, and
the pawing of the war-horse as the warriors of old, in
all their pomp and pride, passed along the unsavoury
thoroughfare, at times on missions of peace, and at
other times when the grim dogs of war had been let
loose, and destruction, rapine, and blood overspread this
fair mountain land of ours. Let us now look at some
of the present-day denizens of the street. Across the

way on the right hand side is the shop of Mr.
Mason, jeweller, whose skill in making Highland ornaments is well and widely known. There he stands
behind the counter, while conversing with him is Mr.
Fraser, the laird of Achnagairn, who is a frequent
visitor to his shop. The next, further along on the
same side, is that of Mr. Goodair, hatter. Observe that
strange sign he has over his doorway—a life size representation of a beaver. Mr. Goodair is not, so far as I
know, a native of the land of the beaver, but all the
same he undertakes to provide " beavers " for the heads
of the community. That gentleman who is standing in
his shop door talking to him is Mr. Morrison, bookseller,
whose establishment ·is on the opposite side of the
street. Dullness of trade and the prospect of a hard
winter is the subject of their conversation, as I can
gather from a remark which has just escaped the lips of
Mr. Goodair. Just below Mr. Morrison's shop is that
of Mr. Dougald M'Queen, shoemaker, who is having a
talk with Councillor Andrew Fraser, who is also in the
trade, being a leather cutter. Both gentlemen are of
the stern old burgher school, where might was considered
as right, and although they may differ on some points,
they certainly agree on one, and that is that there is
nothing like leather. Right opposite Mr. Fraser's shop
is ex-Bailie Lyon's place of business. He is a hardware
merchant, also a tin and copperplate worker, and his
trade is a most extensive one. One of the principal
branches of his establishment is the coppersmith department, from which many distillers, legal and illegal,
in the Highlands are provided with the necessary
producing utensils. If I mistake not it was ex-Bailie
Lyon who in the early part of the century was the
means of getting the charter of the burgh suspended for
several years. During the term of suspension it was

ruled by a Commission appointed by the Court of
Session. There is the ex-Bailie himself; and a stern,
unflinching old man he is, conversing with Mr. James
Suter, who was one of the founders of the *Inverness
Courier*, and who is the leading local historian. Mr.
Suter is one of the good old class of Invernessians, although he is considered by some people to be somewhat
parsimonious. On the opposite side of the street from
Bailie Lyon's shop is the "wee shoppie" of Lachie
M'Intosh, the barber. Let us take a peep in at the
window and see how he and his customers are getting
along. I can hardly make out who that man is he is
operating on in the meantime, the lower part of his
face being simply one huge mass of lather, reminding
me of the remains of a snowdrift beneath some butting
crag. Ah! I might have known who it was; that lofty
brow, those striking features, and that wealth of iron
grey hair are those of Mr. Thomas Mackenzie, the
newly-appointed schoolmaster of the Free Church
Institution. That entry on the same side of the street
is Ross' Close, which is called after the proprietor of
the buildings, Mr. Kenneth Ross. There he is, that
stooping figure, coming up the close. I may mention
that although well up in years he is still in a state of
single blessedness, but it appears to me as if he would
be none the worse of having some tidy, thrifty body to
look after his household affairs. That gentleman who
has just stepped up from behind and is now talking to
him is Mr. Gellon, who is the lessee of the hotel in the
close further up, which hostelry is, by-the-by, a great
rendezvous of the Town-Council, and if the truth be,
told, a good deal of their work is done there. Let us
move on now. That dining-room to the left is the
establishment of Mr. Charles Spinks, who has recently
started business here. Look, at his door is a live

turtle, which is placed there by way of advertisement, and is intended to satisfy the epicurean palates of those who can afford the luxury of turtle soup. Would you mind being treated by me to a plate of the same to-morrow? or perhaps one of Chisholm's Petty Street pies would suit our taste and my pocket better. There are Major Houston, Castlehill, and Mr. Fraser, Torbreck, two well-known local gentlemen, about to enter, while that other gentleman who has just met them on his way out and bowed to them is Captain White of Monar. That building with the steps in front of the main door and the area beneath is the branch office of the National Bank, which is presided over by Mr. M'Kay (Banker M'Kay). There he is standing on the steps conversing with Mr. Peter Anderson, solicitor. Mr. M'Kay, in addition to being bank-agent, is County Fiscal, so that his time is pretty much taken up. Both Mr. Anderson and he are excellent business men, and held in the highest repute by all classes of the community. Directly opposite the bank is the spacious building belonging to the Stewards of the Northern Meeting, the lower part of which is occupied by the extensive drapery business of Mr. Thomas Smith, and is known as the Hunt Hall. Mr. Smith is standing just inside the doorway talking to his brother-in-law, Mr. M'Ewen. That narrow thoroughfare to the right is Baron Taylor's Lane, which derives its name from a factor named Taylor, who was also a "Baron Bailie," and who lived there about the year 1750. On the left hand side leading down towards the river is Bank Lane. In that house at the head of the lane is the workshop of Mr. Finlay Munro, tailor. He has just come down to the door after Kenny M'Lean, an apprentice, whom he has sent for a pound of No. 5 candles for the workshop—his usual order. Listen, he is telling him to be sure to

go to Couborough's on Bridge Street for them, as he
imagines, and perhaps correctly, that he keeps the
best. Big Jimmie M'Pherson, the mail coach guard, has
now got into conversation with Finlay, o'er whose
usually solemn and even cross countenance a benign
smile suddenly seems to play. Ah! I see the reason,
Jimmie is doing "the good Samaritan" by offering to
treat, and both are now making a bee-line up the "Black
Vennel." That shop just beyond the lane was until a few
years ago the Post Office, and as you can observe, it is
rather a small place. Right across is Hodge the
cutler's, and next door is the "London Boot Shop,"
occupied by Bailie M'Kenzie, while on the left hand
side is Mr. Naughtin the jeweller's shop. This gentleman is famed for his excellent workmanship, while his
collection of native Highland ornaments is unsurpassed.
Next door to Naughtin's is the coach office. There it
is with two steps leading up to it. Inside the doorway
are Mr. Elgin, the chief clerk, and Mr. James
M'Pherson, solicitor, whose fine presence and bluff
jovial demeanour and hearty style of conversation is
always refreshing. Both gentlemen are evidently
talking over some local topic, possibly the forthcoming
"walk" of the masonic brethren. This particular
part of the town may be said to be the spot which
connects it with the outer world, for here we have not
only the coach office but the Canal steamers office, and
the Moray Firth Steam Navigation Company's office,
the two latter being on the opposite side of the street,
and close to Ettles Court, a small lane which was once
the connection between Church Street and New Street.
Inside the court is the warehouse of Mr. John Fraser,
auctioner ("Johnnie Merchant"). That tall handsome
man who has just come out of the entrance, and with smart
military step is making his way up Church Street, is

Mr. Fraser, who in his youthful days was in His Majesty's (George IV.) service, and attained the rank of sergeant in that famous regiment, "The Scots Fusilier Guards." That large and commodious building directly opposite is the world-famed hostelry known as the Caledonian Hotel, which is under the able and efficient management of Mr. John Grant. To see this establishment at its busiest we would require to be here in the second week of July, during the progress of the great Wool Fair, and also in September, during the Northern Meeting week. The hotel has been for many years the home of St. John's Kilwinning Lodge of Freemasons (No. 6 of Scotland), a lodge which I have no hesitation in saying is one of the most influential in the country. Mr. Grant, the lessee of the house, has just come out of the shop of our old friend Mr. Archibald Tait, perfumer and hairdresser, and is now hurriedly crossing the pavement towards the entrance of his establishment. Inside Mr. Tait's shop his two sons are busily engaged attending to customers. The second door further down is the old town mansion of Lady Duff of Drummuir, an estate in Banffshire. It was in this house that Prince Charles lived during the occupation of Inverness by himself and his troops in the spring of 1746, it being the only house in the town which had a room without a bed. Of course such an apartment he could not well do without, seeing he had so many receptions. One has only to tax his imagination for a moment, and before him in martial array will appear the shades of the once mighty warriors of the ill-starred Prince as they held high revelry within those ancient walls. After the fateful battle which obliterated for ever the star of the house of Stuart, the youthful commander of the Royalist army presented himself at this mansion, and was shown through the rooms by Lady Drummuir, who

N

said to him, "Here are the apartments just recently
occupied by your Highness' royal cousin, Charles
Edward." The duration of Cumberland's stay in town was
probably about a week, and it may possibly have been in
this mansion that Duncan Forbes of Culloden remon-
strated with him for his brutality, while at the same time
pointing out to him that there were laws in this country
for the protection of the people. The Duke's reply was
characteristic, "Aye, but I will show them what brigade
law is." That ecclesiastical edifice of gothic design.
and with unfinished tower on the opposite side of the
street is the Scotch Episcopal Church, dedicated to St.
John. It is presided over by Dean Fyvie, who is an
able and eloquent divine, and who is much respected
by his people. This building was erected some years
ago to take the place of a chapel which was situated on
this street, and almost opposite the High Church gate,
but which has now been demolished. The buildings
adjoining the chapel are, as you will observe, of the
eighteenth century type, and are occupied by a highly
respectable class of tenants. Mr. James Sharp, tailor,
a quiet and unobtrusive citizen, occupies one of the
flats. There he is about to enter the court, while his
fellow-craftsman, Mr. Alexander M'Bean, has just hailed
him. They have entered into conversation which is
doubtless relative to guildry matters, the latter being
deacon of his own craft. Both men are excellent
tradesmen and highly intelligent, taking a great interest
in all matters pertaining to the welfare of their fellow-
townsmen. That plain substantial-looking building
next door to the court is the Royal Hotel, of which Mr.
M'Donell is lessee. For many years it has been the
resort of commercial men and middle-class tourists.
That house further down the street with triangular
sculptured stones over the top windows, bearing

certain emblems and initials, with the date 1700, and entered by a close which is known as "Abertarff's Close," is now occupied by tradespeople, but was at one time the residence of aristocratic families, and the interior of the rooms still bear indication of former grandeur. On the left hand side of the street and a little further along is the shop of Mr. M'Lennan, watchmaker. This gentleman visited London some time ago and selected the fine bell of the West Church, as well as the handsome clock in the interior thereof. He and his wife have just emerged from the shop and are making their way to their home at Porterfield, while that distinguished-looking clerical gentleman who has met them, and to whom they are talking, is the Rev. Mr. Clark, who, as you will remember, I pointed out to you recently on the opposite side of the river. Mrs. Maclennan is a London lady, and is sister to the celebrated Dr. Halley, Congregational minister of Manchester. She is herself a lady of outstanding ability, and is an eloquent exponent of the temperance cause. A little further along on the same side of the street is the shop of Mr. Fraser, leather merchant, who, owing to his complexion, is known as "The White Laad." That man entering the doorway is a customer, a well-known local son of St. Crispin, who goes by the name of "Jock Fixey," and meeting Mr. Fraser they are having a "confab." Hark! Jock is saying, "There will soon be no shoemakers at all; machinery will do the whole work, and they will have nothing to do but throw the leather into the machine, and out the boots'll come by the gross." That wide street to the left running west is Fraser Street, which has derived its name from ex-Provost Fraser ("Buchty"), but of it anon. Almost directly opposite is the handsome town residence of Raigmore, the portico of which, as you see, reaches out beyond the pavement. To the rear is an immense garden, the huge back wall of which I pointed out to you while we strolled down New Street some time ago. That trim well-knit gentleman with the frock coat and tall white hat is Mr. William Smith, watchmaker, whose shop, as you will observe, is situated on the ground floor of Raigmore's mansion. Mr. Smith is also an optician of some merit, and the telescope which he so jauntily holds under his arm is his own construction. He has just returned from his favourite stroll round the Longman, where, by the aid of his glass, he is able to take note of whatever ships may be making their way up the firth. Mr. Smith is, if we mistake not, the oldest tradesman in the street, his business being com-menced in 1805. That business-looking building right across the way with trees in front is the Commercial Bank. Mr. Wilson is the local agent. See, there he is standing on the pavement in front of the bank, convers-ing with Mr. Charles Stewart, solicitor, and Mr. Joseph Mitchell, C.E., Inspector of Highland Roads and Bridges. You ask if that tall eccentric-looking gentleman coming along, wearing the long blue semi-military cloak, and tightly grasping the massive iron-shod walking stick, is a Spanish general or some foreign potentate. No, that is Æneas Mackintosh of Dalmigavie, who is registrar of sasines, and whose office is a few doors down. The most of the buildings on the left hand side for a considerable distance are offices and dwelling-houses, while behind are long stretches of gardens leading towards Bank Street. That shop with the steps leading down to the floor, and the fine specimens of plain and fancy wicker work displayed in the low windows, is the shop of Mr. Joseph Marello, who has recently commenced business in town, and whose wares, useful and ornamental, are much appreciated by his many customers. Mr. Marello is a native of the city of Genoa, and judging from the warm interest he is taking in the affairs of the town of his adoption, it may be easy to conclude that he has come to stay. That building to the right with area and steps leading up to the main door is the house of Dr. Roderick Fraser ("Rory Buich"). He is just coming along the street accompanied by Mr. Angus Mackintosh, the young Laird of Holm. Like the other medicals in town, Dr. Fraser is a particularly handsome gentleman. A striking contrast to Raigmore's mansion and Dr. Fraser's residence are the small houses and shops to the right. These form perhaps the last remaining link with the business establishments of the long-gone past, and are indicative of the class of shops which used to exist in Inverness many years ago. The houses are, as you can see, exceedingly ancient in design, and much sunk below the level of the roadway, while the places of business to the front gable are, to say the least, neither elegant, commodious, nor extensive. The windows, as you will observe, are conspicuous by their absence, so that the display of wares is not elaborate, while the entrances, which are on "the barn-door" plan, look exceedingly quaint. There is Mr. Paterson, the butcher leaning over the lower part of his door (which is of course closed), enjoying his smoke and talking to Mr. Fraser next door, who is also in the same attitude, while the top door of the next shop is closed, indicating that the proprietor is meanwhile absent from business. In all probability it was in one of these houses right in the close from the shops that Flora Macdonald and her young daughter lodged in 1780 during their stay in Inverness. There is such a mine of interesting information connected with Church Street, and so many objects of interest still to describe, that I think it would not be wise

to attempt a further description this evening, so we will
accordingly retrace our steps and resume at this point
when we meet next.

NOTE.—Owing to the comparatively long distance,
and the inconvenience of travelling to the more central
and fashionable cities in the south, social intercourse
was for a long time a much-felt want by the resident
gentry and the landed proprietors in the vicinity of
Inverness. To remedy the very apparent necessity, it
was resolved after due consideration to hold an annual
society gathering at Inverness in the spring of the
year. This was the inception of what has been known
for over a century as the " Northern Meeting," the first
of which was held in May 1788, and usually lasted
nearly a week. The stewards engaged the best hotels
in town, each hotel being occupied by the guests for a
day. Breakfast being partaken of, the time was
as agreeably spent as possible till dinner was served,
which was a sumptuous one. The ladies thereafter
retired to the drawing-rooms, the gentlemen enjoying
the usual after-dinner speeches until it was time to
dress for the assembly, which took place in the evening.
The " Meeting" was much appreciated not only by those
who had the privilege of participating therein, but
also by the tradespeople, and by those who had
apartments to let in town. The attendance at the
meetings continued to increase every year, until the
stewards found it necessary to get the present handsome building erected, where it still stands near the top
of Church Street. It is recorded that in 1805 a serious
fire broke out in the building. The Justiciary Court
being held at the time in the town, the presiding
judge, Lord Gardenstone, who was lodged in the house,
having a narrow escape. The cook-maid heroically

carried the Judge on her back through the flames to a place of safety. For her presence of mind she was awarded a pension for life. The fire having taken place on a Saturday night, tailors were employed all Sunday to replenish his Lordship's wardrobe by Monday. At the earlier Meetings several nice points were raised, perhaps having reference to the feudal times, particularly the order of precedence being strictly adhered to. The most ancient family in the neighbourhood being represented by Mr. Robertson of Inshes. That gentleman, along with his family and relations, had for many years claimed the privilege of being the first to ascend the stairs and enter the ballroom. The Meeting was honoured by a visit from H. R. H. The Prince Consort in August 1847. If I mistake not it was in the early thirties that piping and dancing and Highland games was introduced as part of the programme of the Meeting. The games took place in the Academy Park, where a large enclosure was set up, including a spacious grand stand for the accommodation of the visitors. The sports commenced at two o'clock in the afternoon. Shortly after one o'clock our old friends, Sergeants Tallach and Chisholm, with capacious canvas bags fastened round their waists, took up their positions on each side of the gate, and received a shilling from each entrant, which was the uniform charge for a seat in the grand stand. Sergeant Grant ("Supple") was meantime stationed at a small door in the back wall of the park, and admitted the humbler members of the community to the show for the small sum of threepence, while many of the younger folks were allowed to pass in free, when they had the privilege of standing where best they could. The distance from the hotels being short, no carriages were necessary. It was very interesting to see the continuous

stream of handsome and fashionably-dressed ladies and
gentlemen walking along High Street and Inglis Street
and the usually quiet thoroughfare of New Street on
their way to the park (there being no Union
Street at the time we write of), the majority of the
gentlemen being attired in the Highland garb. In 1888
the stewards very handsomely commemorated the
centenary of the Meeting by furnishing a ward in
the Infirmary, which was handed over to the trustees,
the same to be known for all time as the " Northern
Meeting Ward." The small shop with a few steps
leading down to it at the top of Bank Lane, with the
entrance from the lane, was until recent years occupied
as the Post Office, there being one apartment, and
in the window facing the street was placed the slit
for receiving the letters, measuring four inches by a
quarter of an inch, there being no need for any larger.
The officials consisted of the Postmaster and the
letter carrier. There being no regular postal service
to the country districts, the letter carrier used to go
to the Exchange on market days with whatever letters
he had for the country, and lustily call out the names
of those to whom letters were addressed, and would
at once hand the letters to any who chose to claim
them, provided they paid the postage. Previous to
1840 there was a scale of charges for letters one
quarter of an ounce in weight, 1s. 6d. to or from
London and 3d. to Beauly. Dean Fyvie, who for many
years presided with much acceptance over the congregation worshipping in St. John's Episcopal Church,
died in 1849, and was interred in the Chapel Yard,
close to the street boundary wall, beside the grave of
Bishop Andrew MacFarlane (his father-in-law) of the
Diocese of Moray and Ross, and that of the Rev.
James Hay, formerly a minister of the Scottish Episcopal

Church in Inverness, who died in 1758, in the twenty-fourth year of his ministry. During the demolition in 1846 of the old house 46 Church Street, formerly occupied by Lady Duff of Drummuir, a quantity of muskets and swords, which in all probability belonged to the period of the "45," was found concealed in a recess at the back part of the building. The watch-making business to which I have referred as being carried on by Mr. Smith, and subsequently by his son Robert, is still efficiently conducted by our esteemed townsman, Mr. Alexander Dallas. The business has just attained its century. Dr. Fraser, to whom I have referred, removed, if I mistake not, for the benefit of his health with his family to Florence, from which city during his lifetime he kept in touch with his many friends in Inverness. I had the pleasure of the acquaintance of one of the doctor's sons, Mr. Samuel Westcott, who was for some time an zealous member of the Inverness Noetic Society, and for some time attended the University of St. Andrews.

CHAPTER XXXI.

CHURCH STREET (*continued*)—HIGH CHURCH AND CHURCH
YARD—GAELIC CHURCH.

OUR progress through the town recently has been
somewhat slow, the reason being, as I already told you,
that I was desirous of pointing out and explaining
everything of interest along our route. Of all the
thoroughfares in our ancient and royal burgh Church
Street is perhaps the most interesting, and I know you
will therefore pardon me for again returning to it this
afternoon. We will accordingly adjourn to the spot
where we stopped short the other day. This is it, if I
mistake not (opposite the old world shops), and that is
the establishment of Mr. Henry Tough, painter and
decorator, on the west side of the street. Mr. Tough
is a well-known business man in town, and being an
excellent mechanic, he is much sought after in connection
with house decorations. There he is coming out of the shop
of Mr. Robert Imrie, cabinetmaker, which is next door.
The latter gentleman has accompanied him to the door,
and they are evidently having a talk over some business
matter. Mr. Imrie is a gentleman of the good old type,
and one has only to look at his portly figure, smiling,
affable countenance, and listen to the clear ring of his
voice to realise at once that he is a man who is the
friend of all. Directly opposite Mr. Imrie's shop is the
recently opened establishment of Calder, also a cabinetmaker. He is just despatching some furniture and helping
to get it loaded on to a hurley. Mr. George Urquhart,

tailor, has stepped up and is giving him a hand to get
an armchair properly set on the vehicle. Mr. Urquhart
is in business in his own trade, and, in good old-
fashioned style, believes in giving a helping hand to a
neighbour. That archway several yards further down
is known as "The Bow Court," and leads to the
residence of the Rev. Mr. Clark and Mr. Peter Scott
of the Academy. This building replaced the former
residence of Lady Duff of Drummuir, which was demolished in 1722. In the lane round the corner
is the Trades Hall, which was until recently the meeting
place of the six incorporated trades in town. That
substantial antique-looking building just beyond the
lane is Dunbar's Hospital, and is reckoned to be one of
the oldest structures in town, as you will observe from
the quaint sculptured windows, crow stepped gables,
and old-fashioned gateway in the lane. It has in its
time served not a few purposes, and has recently been
opened as the parochial poorhouse for the parish, and
is in charge of Mr. Alexander Fraser, who it is said
makes the inmates feel quite at home, notwithstanding the fact that institutions of this kind are not
always considered to be of the most hospitable
character. We are now opposite the shop of Mr.
Logan, plumber, whose supply of lead is stored in the
recess formed by the abutting gable of the hospital.
This gentleman is just directing two of his men, who
are measuring and cutting some lead in connection with
a building contract at which they are engaged. Mr.
Slorah, woodturner, has just come up and entered into
conversation with Mr. Logan, while these four charming
daintily-attired little girls, who have come tripping
lightly out of that doorway, are the daughters of the
latter. I need hardly tell you what that gateway on
the opposite side of the street is. It is the entrance

leading into the High Church and Churchyard. Let us step in for a few minutes, as I see the gate stands wide open. The prominent and still handsomely carved burying-place to the right is that of the Robertsons of Inshes, while all around sleep many of the once influential citizens of Inverness, as well as they who could not in their time lay claim to much of the wealth of the earth. Let us now enter, and in doing so our attention is at once attracted to the many beautifully carved monuments, adorned with figures and crests in high relief, which are placed in the aisles and on the inner walls of the church. You will observe that, with the exception of the magisterial pew in the front gallery, the interior, so far as the seating is concerned, is anything but comfortable, while the "decorations" are *nil*, strongly reminding one of the remark made by a Highlander while present at a festival at St. Peter's in Rome, who said, " In my country they worship the Lord like a beggar, but here they worship Him like a gentleman." No doubt, as time goes on, there will be improvements in the interior. Here is Mr. James Anderson, doorkeeper. " Hullo, James, how are you getting along?" " Oh, fine, I'm just trying to keep the old place in order, lad ; Dr. Rose likes to see it kept as trim as possible." " Thomas Grant the beadle will be about, I suppose." " Yes there he comes ; he was just up in the library dusting some books." " How do you do, Mr. Grant, and how are you liking your new job ? " " Oh, I like it up to the mark. My friend James and I will soon get the place into shipshape." " You don't belong to Inverness, Mr. Grant ? " " No, I came from Cromarty." " You'll not have Gaelic then." " No ; there is very little Gaelic spoken there. I came to Inverness when I was quite young, previous to which I was in farm service. D'ye know I've often heard my earliest master (who was an old man) say that he was the first farmer in the district who raised the ploughmen's wages to £1 in the half-year (including meal, milk, &c.). When I came to Inverness I started the heckling down at the Sconce, and although I was poorly paid, I preferred it to farm work, which is a most slavish job." "You will consider yourself quite an Invernessian now, Mr. Grant." "Oh, quite. I am a long time here now, and taking everything into consideration, I haven't got on so bad; between town-guard night duty, and work about the church, I manage to make ends meet wonderfully, considering that I have a big family to bring up." "It's a fine old building the tower of the church." "It is that. I daresay it is the oldest in Inverness, and is likely to stand for many years yet, but the clock is in bad condition; indeed, it hasn't gone for many years, and is an eyesore to the public, for you know there are few things so wearisome as to be always looking at a time-piece that never moves." "You are the bellringer?" "I am, and a driech job it is. Just fancy coming in here at five in the morning in the dead of winter for the purpose of awakening the drowsy breadwinners." "The dead won't trouble you much, I suppose." "Indeed no! they are very quiet neighbours, but occasionally I meet some drunken fellows who have been out on the spree all night, and they are as a rule ugly customers to come across." "How many bells are there?" "Two, and one of them is of considerable antiquity, being at one time in the tower of the old Fortrose Cathedral." "Oh, by-the-by, Mr. Grant, could you point out the spot in the Churchyard where the poor Highlanders captured at Culloden were shot?" "Just come along with me. It is nearly halfway between the boundary wall and the west porch." (Walks in the direction indicated.) "Here is the fatal place, lads, and every time I come near it I seem to hear the crack of the musket, the groans of the dying, and see the ugly leer on the face of the Hanoverian officer, as in merciless tones he utters his cruel command. It was terrible work; just fancy the poor fellows, some of them sick and wounded, taken from the Gaelic Church over there, which was used as a temporary hospital, and launched into eternity to please the whim of Cumberland, the bloodthirsty scoundrel." "Thank you for your valuable information; you are quite an authority on such matters, Tom." "Oh, I know a good deal about these things, but my predecessor, 'Little Simony,' was better versed than me. He could have told you lots of interesting stories about the church and its surroundings. I remember him telling me that when he was a young man he heard the great John Wesley and the no less distinguished Principal Baird, of Edinburgh, preach here. One thing that struck him in connection with these clerics was that they wore the old-fashioned breeches, silk stockings, shoes, and buckles, as he himself did up to the last." "We will now take a step along to the Gaelic Church, which in its own way is quite as interesting as its more pretentious neighbour here." "Just so; you will find Adam MacBain ("Addy"), the beadle there, and he will tell you what he knows. Good day, then." "Good day, Tom." Having seen all that is of interest here, we will now stroll down to St. Mary's Gaelic Church. Here it is, this plain-looking building. You will notice that in the centre of the building a doorway has been built up, indicating that at one time the vestry was here, and I see the main door is open, so we will just take the same liberties here as we did at the High Church. There is Adam sweeping out the passages. "Well, Adam, how are you getting along?" "Oh, not so

bad. A'm just trying to kick up a bit of a dust.
Phew! Atchoo! Atchoo!" "That's a great pulpit,
Addy," "It iss chust a great pulpit: so they say
whatever, but if they had the cleaning of it, they
wouldna think so much o't. They say that it was
carved by a herd lad at Culloden. A'ch but it's a
gran work whatever, and him must hev been a clever
laddie." "Oh, indeed, the work of a herd-boy. It just
looks like that." "Yes, and they say that wan pin keeps
it together, but I could never find it." "I daresay
not, Addy. That's the trades loft up there?" "It iss,
but there's no many trades come to it noo, since the
people left the church, especially to the English; Mr.
MacPherson sometimes preaches to gey empty pews,
but perhaps they'll come back yet." "Well, good
evening, we'll not be keeping you from your work any
longer." "Good night" (resumes his brushing). We
will now move farther down, and have at length
reached the junction of Church Street and Chapel
Street. At the head of Chapel Street and to the right
are the Monumental Works of Mr. John Batchen,
who is recognised as one of the first tradesmen in his
line in the north. An active and intelligent business
man, he is also an enthusiastic freemason, and is held in
high respect by the entire community. The art of stone
engraving is doubtless an old one in town, as is
evidenced by the admirably executed stones and
monuments in the various burial places. Talking on this subject reminds me that there are some
curious stories told of old-time local stone engravers.
One is to the effect that a stonecutter was cutting the
following text on a tombstone in the chapel yard,
" A virtuous woman is a crown to her husband," and
that, being possibly troubled about the domestic
financial exchequer, he absent-mindedly made the

quotation read, "A virtuous woman is a 5s. to her husband." Perhaps he was not so far wrong after all. That tall young lad who is busily engaged inside Mr. Batchen's yard smoothing a stone is Donald Davidson, who is said to have a special aptitude for the trade. Right across from Mr. Batchen's gate is the meal shop of John Sutherland ("Big John"). There he is coming up Chapel Street as white as a miller, and that handsome business-looking gentleman whom he has just stopped to talk to is Mr. Rose, baker, and they are doubtless discussing the probability of a rise in the price of grain as the season advances. We will now turn down Friars' Lane in the direction of the Ness. At the corner on our left are the byres, stables, &c. of Mr. Frank Fraser, who rents a considerable portion of land in the vicinity of the Longman. While directly opposite Mr. Fraser's steading is the residence of Mrs. Fraser, Lakefield, who is standing in her doorway bidding good afternoon to her medical adviser, Dr. Manford. As there is nothing further of particular note in this lane, and as we have already explored the region to the right, we will make our way to Bank Street. We are now at the riverside. That neat and somewhat pretentious row of residences along the bank, leading in the direction of the Maggot, is Douglas Row. I could never exactly find out how it came by that name, but possibly it was called after the man who built the first house on the street, who, for aught I know, may have been a descendant of the Black Douglas of Scottish history. It is now getting too dark to proceed farther on our "tour of investigation," so we will cease from our wanderings for the day. Indeed, now that I think of it, we might well afford to discontinue our walks until the spring of the year, seeing we have already taken in the most of the town. The weather at this season is not at all pleasant for sight seeing, and as I should like you to have a favourable impression of our good town, I would prefer that our final walks be in the season when nature arouses herself from her long wintry sleep, and dons her vernal garb.

NOTE.—Dunbar's Hospital was erected by Provost Alexander Dunbar in the year 1662, and left in charge of the presbytery and kirk-session of the parish of Inverness. I presume that the building was intended for the shelter and care of the aged and helpless poor of the town, which purpose I believe it amply fulfilled, as well as many purposes of the kind in its time. On the accession of William III. to the British throne in 1688 there came over with the king an officer named Albert Sleazer, who subsequently received the appointment of Master Gunner for Scotland. Being of an artistic turn, he requested permission from the king to sketch His Majesty's towns and cities in Scotland, to be engraved and embodied in a handsome portfolio. This work he achieved with great care and at considerable personal expense. His view of Inverness is dated 1693, and is the earliest known view of the town. In this view is shown a small dome surmounting the roof of Dunbar's Hospital. In the sketch prominence is given to the square tower, steeple, and church (now known as the High Church). The eminence on which this church is built has been known in bygone ages as St. Michael's Hill. The tower of the church, I understand, is of great antiquity, while the burying-ground has no doubt been the scene of many a civil and historic function. In the "Life of Dr. Alexander Lindsay, Moderator of the General Assembly of the Church of Scotland," we read that when the Covenant was sent to Inverness to be

O

signed the burghers were summoned by "tuck of drum" to the churchyard for that purpose. The report adds that the Provost (he being no doubt a Jacobite) was not expected to turn up, but if not, he would have "a thin back." Toward the middle of the eighteenth century the church fell into disrepair, and remained for many years unoccupied, the pulpit being used as a sleeping place by an eccentric character known as the "ministear na feusaig" (the bearded minister), he wearing an unusual long beard. Toward the close of the century the session set about restoring the building in such a manner as to accommodate the congregation for nearly another century. It was usual for a Highland regiment of the auxiliary forces to be stationed at Inverness, and on Sundays the men attended Divine Service in Gaelic in the chapelyard, there being no accommodation for them in the Parish Church. The matter was made known to Queen Anne, and Her Majesty expressed sympathy for her Highland soldiers, and gave instructions for the present Gaelic Parish Church to be built, while sufficient provision for the support of the ministry was secured by a gift of land situated in Morayshire for that purpose. The carved pulpit which has been associated with the history of the church was in all probability brought over by some benevolent-minded burgher from Holland. My grandmother used to relate that when she was a girl she saw the pulpit in many pieces in the river at the foot of Friars' Lane undergoing a thorough cleaning. Before leaving the subject of the churches, I may state that the Rev. John Wesley visited Inverness four times, the first visit taking place in 1764, when Mr. Wesley writes, under date Sunday, 10th June, "At ten I went to the kirk. After service Mr. Fraser, one of the ministers, invited us to dinner and then to drink tea. As we were drinking tea, he asked at what hour I would please to preach. I said at half-past five o'clock. The High Kirk was filled in a very short time, and I have seldom found greater liberty of spirit. The other minister came afterwards to our inn and showed the most cordial affection. . . . . All I could do was to preach once more at Inverness. I think the church was fuller now than before, and I could not but observe the remarkable behaviour of the whole congregation after service. Neither man, woman, or child spoke one word all the way down the main street. Indeed, the seriousness of the people is the less surprising when it is considered that for at least a hundred years this town has had such a succession of pious ministers as very few in Great Britain have known. After Edinburgh, Glasgow, and Aberdeen, I think Inverness the largest town I have seen in Scotland. The main streets are broad and straight, the houses mostly old but not very bad, none very good. It stands in a pleasant and fruitful country, and has all things needful for life and godliness. The people in general speak remarkably good English, and are of a friendly, courteous behaviour." Again Mr. Wesley writes, Tuesday, May 11th, 1784, " Notwithstanding the long discontinuance of morning preaching, we had a large congregation at five. I breakfasted at the first house I was invited to at Inverness, where good Mr. Mackenzie then lived. His three daughters live in it now, one of whom inherits all the spirit of her father. In the afternoon we took a walk over the bridge into one of the pleasantest countries I have seen. It runs along by the side of the clear river, and is well cultivated and well wooded, and here first we heard abundance of birds welcoming the return of spring."

CHAPTER XXXII.

BANK STREET—"COURIER" OFFICE—NESS BANK—THE
HAUGH—VIEW PLACE.

THE long night of winter being now over, and the
atmospheric conditions more congenial than when we
last parted, we will have a better opportunity of bringing to a close what has proved to be an exceedingly
interesting and enjoyable "perambulation" through
this our ancient town. Our course may have been
somewhat labyrinthian and our pace somewhat snail-
like, but we have the satisfaction of knowing that we
daundered about with our eyes wide open. Since last
we met at this spot in dark December there have been
many strange happenings in Inverness, while trade has
been dull, work scarce, food dear, and the poor have
consequently heard the angry howl of the wolf at the
door. Many good citizens and true "have shuffled off
this mortal coil," and the land as usual has been draped
in white, while the ice king held it in his iron grasp.
Now, with the advent of spring, "the scene is changed,"
trade is reviving, the health-giving zephyr comes as an
elixir to the weak and ailing affected by the wintry
blast. The birds are singing and the trees are budding,
indicating that the gloom of winter has lifted. If I
remember correctly it was exactly at this point (the
foot of Friars' Lane) that we brought our last walk to a
close. So we will now move up Bank Street. The
river is pretty high, and as there is no embankment, it
threatens to "invade the cottages." There is, how-

ever, room enough on the roadway to enable us to pass by dry-shod. One of the cottages is occupied by Mr. Burgess, saddler, an excellent old citizen, who is smoking his evening pipe at the door, and from the anxious look on his face, he is evidently concerned about the progress the tide is making. Some of the other occupants of the street also seem "put about," while away down at Douglas Row yonder the water is half-way across the road. Indeed, so far as this par- ticular spot is concerned, it would be very much better from a sanitary point of view if the river was always at its present height, the reason being that the main sewer has its outlet into the foot of Church Lane. We need hardly say that the effluvium which proceeds from it when the river is low is not so pleasant to inhale as the odour of the attar of roses. That large garden on the south side of the lane, with trees over- hanging the wall, seems to me to be a most suitable site for some important edifice, and I should not be at all surprised to see one erected there. Just fancy how imposing a stately spire would look here, with its state- liness reflected in the crystal waters at its base ! Some distance further up the street is the house of Miss Kennedy, a most highly respected lady, whose abode is well known for its hospitality, it being the favourite residence of genteel families who visit town for short periods. A few steps beyond Miss Kennedy's house is Mr. Macfarquhar's "smiddy," which, as I think I told you before, was erected early in the century as an Independent chapel for the Rev. James Kennedy. Next door is the building in course of construction as a place of worship for the recently formed Free High Church congregation in Inverness. That establishment which occupies the space between the new building and Mr. Kennedy's present church is Mr. Fraser's coach-

work. Having now reached the foot of Fraser Street,
let us have a look at the old brewery, which ceased
operations some few years ago, its worthy proprietor,
Provost John Fraser, having along with his family
emigrated to Canada. What bill is that on the
entrance? Let us go over and see. Ah, ha! Well,
well! They've turned the old place into a museum
now. Listen! " A strange fish recently caught by the
fishers at Petty. To be seen within. Admission twopence." I feel certain that this is not the first strange
fish that came from Petty, although it is perhaps the
first that has been on exhibition from that neighbourhood. Charging twopence for seeing it is a new way of
levying " petty " customs. It may be a curious enough
fish all the same, but I don't think we should go in
to-day to see it. Doesn't it occur to you as a remarkable coincidence that a stranded ichthyological specimen
should find its way into an establishment which once
manufactured a concoction which slaked the mouths of
many who were reputed to be " as thirsty as fish"? Let
us dodge along now. There is the entrance to the
Caledonian Stables, and some of the " strappers," as
you see, are busy giving the horses a rub down, while
others are cleaning the coaches. That narrow thoroughfare running to the left in the direction of Church
Street is Bank Lane, which I pointed out to you as we
passed down Church Street. On the north corner of
the lane is the Caledonian Stables hay-loft, while that
substantial-looking building on the south corner is
perhaps one of the most important edifices in town,
for it is no less than the office from which emanates
one of the few influential public prints published
in Scotland, *The Inverness Courier*, whose first issue
dates as far back as 1817. We will step in and
have a look round for a few minutes. Although

it is publication day, Mr. George Wood, the manager, who is ever affable and courteous, will not object, I feel certain. (Enter the office and meet Mr. Wood.) "Good day, Mr. Wood; we just took a look in as we heard you had got some new machinery." "Yes, and it is a great help to us, for it enables us to get on with the printing very much quicker. The composing is of course necessarily a slow job, but possibly, as time goes on, that may even be improved on. Just go down and take a look through the machine-room. Andrew Dunlop is down there, and will explain matters to you." (Visit the machine-room.) "Hullo, Andrew, I just came down to show my friend the new printing machine." "Oh, certainly. It is worth seeing, and is an improvement on the old method. It's a pity you could not see it working." "It is a most interesting piece of mechanism, certainly, and we may yet have an opportunity of seeing it. 'printing off,' but meanwhile we will not prolong our visit, as we are detaining you, so we will just bid you 'Good evening,' Andrew." Those two young lads we met on the stair carrying a "forme" are apprentices, their names being Hugh Graham and Willie Mackay. They are both bright young fellows, and will yet get on, I have no doubt. Those other two youths who just entered the editorial rooms are Mr. Carruthers' sons, Robert and Walter, who have called to see their father on their way home from the Academy. He is not in, I can see. Having again got out into the lane, we will turn up the riverside. Here comes the burly form of William Campbell, the *Courier's* collector, mounted on a hardy grey garron. He has evidently just returned from a long journey. Let us converse with him. "It's a beautiful evening, Mr. Campbell; you are just returning after the day's darg." "Yes, I've been up through Glen Urquhart doing some collecting. What delightful weather we are having after the severe winter!" (Mr. Campbell dismounts and addresses two boys standing by.) "Here, Johnnie and Paul Kinnaird, bring this pony round to the stable, and see that he gets a good feed of oats and is properly groomed and bedded for the night." (Paul mounts and rides away triumphantly, while Johnnie follows.) "A pair of nice smart lads. They are passionately fond of horses, and watch my animal regularly. They are sons of Captain Kinnaird, a much esteemed master mariner, who stays in Bank Lane, close to the office. Here comes Mr. Carruthers himself, just returning from lunch, accompanied by no less a personage than Hugh Miller, who, as you are aware, is one of of the greatest literary and scientific geniuses that this, the North Countree, has produced, and has for some time been editing *The Witness* in Edinburgh. Both gentlemen bow to Mr. Campbell, while Mr. Carruthers speaks. "You have got back, William. I hope you have had a successful journey." "An excellent journey, sir." "And you mean to tell us, Mr. Campbell, that that plain-looking countryman with the shaggy locks, the thoughtful countenance, and o'er whose broad shoulders a shepherd's plaid is carelessly slung, is the great Hugh Miller, who by the brilliancy of his genius has made the very stones to speak, and who by his mastery of the pen has performed deeds mightier than the warrior with his sword?" "That is the man, and what he has already done is only but an earnest of what he will yet achieve. You are, I suppose, aware that it was in the *Inverness Courier* that his earliest efforts in prose appeared, being a series of articles on 'The Herring Fishing.' It was Mr. Carruthers who discovered (to use his own words) that 'a great prose writer had arisen in the land,' and as the years go by his faith in the Cromarty stonemason increases. Indeed, as you now see, they are close friends, while the bond of friendship seems to be getting more closely cemented daily. It's time, however, that I was getting into the office to hand over my cash and square up accounts. So I'll be bidding you good-bye at present." "Good-bye, Mr. Campbell, and thank you for your crack." Next door to the *Courier* office is the branch office of the Bank of Scotland, while adjoining it is the Inverness office of Bell, Rannie, and Company, wine merchants, Leith, who are represented by Mr. Hugh Bain, who is also secretary of the Northern Meeting, and is held in high esteem by the aristocracy. Beyond this building are the stables of John Fraser ("Jock Beef"), while close by is the so-called "Queen Mary's House," which we already inspected. Just imagine a reputed royal residence all but turned into a stable. Let us pass the gable of Castle Tolmie and cross over to Ness Walk, and take a stroll up the riverside. There across the way goes two well-known Petty Street sons of St. Crispin, "Jock Spindles" and "Dola Major." They are doubtless making for the garret of old Donald Treasurer over in Davis Square, where a lively discussion will, I feel certain, take place on the terms of the new statement of wages which the craft propose to present to the masters, while Donald's aviary will also receive due attention. We are now treading new ground, and will go up as far as the "Silver Pool" this evening. To the left in all their grandeur rise the Castle and the Castle Hill, but of them anon, while that portion of the river to our right is known as "The Castle Pool" or "Castle Shott," of which mention has previously been made. What horse and trap is this coming tearing along, the animal lashed in foam? Ah, we might have known it is on Her Majesty's service. There is John Macbean, "the messenger," while seated by his side is a prisoner securely handcuffed, "poor fellow." The journey has evidently been a long one, but the gaol or rather the *jail* is nigh, and the latter, whatever his crime, will find lodgings in Bridge Street for the night at least. In front of us lies Ness Bank, while that small triangular green to the left is a favourite playground of the small boys, and the grazing place of pet goats. I need hardly tell you that some exciting encounters take place here, for you know the average billy-goat likes to be monarch of all he surveys, while the light-hearted mischievous lad is inclined to dispute his rights. Hark! 'tis the sound of the pibroch! Here comes a wedding from the Leys district, making for the Rev. David Sutherland's residence at 22 Ness Bank. What a happy party! There goes the bride in all her "braws," while the bridegroom, poor chap, looks quite uncomfortable in his flowered waistcoat, black coat, trousers of the latest cut, and tall silk hat. The remainder of the party are, as you will observe, less conspicuously attired, the older women wearing high dressed caps and tartan shawls, and some of the men old-fashioned suits and ancient-looking head gear that have evidently done similar duty on many occasions. Ness Bank, which we are now traversing, is the favourite residential quarter of prominent Inverness business men. The two gentlemen who have passed us are George and Robert Mackay, grocers, Castle Raat, on their way from dinner. Ah, here come the "Buy-a-Brooms," quite a picturesque and fascinating little group in their way. They are a bevy of Swiss maidens, as their quaint dress indicates, who come here regularly every year at this time to dispose of dusting brushes or brooms for spring cleaning, and as they sell them about from door to door, they attract much attention, not only by their smart attire and pleasant manner, but by the sweet melody of their voices as they chant the praises of their wares. The girls have now separated, and are displaying the brushes at the front doors of different houses as they sing—

"Buy a broom, buy a broom,
Come buy me a broom,
Buy a broom, buy a broom,
Come buy me a broom.
There's one for the lady,
And one for the baby,
And one for the master,
Come buy a broom, O!"

I need hardly say that these children of the Alps are as welcome as the flowers in May. We have at last reached the Silver Pool, which is a favourite fishing ground for local anglers. That new building to the left, of which "the founds" have newly been laid, is to be the manse of the Rev. Joseph Thorburn of the Free Church. We will at this point turn up into The Haugh. Away beyond are the beautiful Ness Islands, which are gradually becoming a popular resort, and will doubtless in the future be looked upon as among the greatest attractions of the town. The few large villas below the hill embedded in foliage are the residences of well-known local gentlemen, and the district is known as Island Bank. On the top edge of the hill there is the Godsman's Walk, which I think I already referred to. That monotonous sound you hear away in the distance is the steady "thump, thump" of the turbine wheel at the water-house near the Islands. Here comes Mr. Macdonald, the water manager, himself, who is familiarly known as "Ewen, the Waterman." His stout well-knit figure, attired in dark moleskin coat of ample dimension, and trousers of the same material, a well-worn silk hat adorning his head, is well known throughout town, and as he goes his daily round, water key in hand, he comes in contact with all classes of the community, who entertain for him the highest respect. See, the key in his hand is like polished silver, which is an indication that it is ever in use. Let us have a word with him in the by-going. "You are getting home, Mr. Macdonald, after your day's work." "Yes, just getting home, and a queer job I have keeping the housewives supplied with water. It is not bad when the river is high, but in the summer it is terrible work. The company will have to make some improvement soon if they mean to keep the town in water. The folk on the hill are very badly off sometimes." "You have one consolation, Mr. Macdonald, anyway, for you are certainly the most indispensable official in the burgh, and without you the townspeople would be ill-off indeed." "Imph! Well, I daresay there's some truth in that too, but that reminds me that I have an important bit of work on to-night yet, so I must be bidding you good-day." We will walk townwards through "The Haugh." On the right is Fraser Street, which is comprised of a few well-kept cottages occupied by work-people. Below the hill is the old-fashioned residence known as Gordonville, which is occupied by Mrs. Inglis, the widow of our late highly-respected Provost. Nearer town is the pig killing and curing establishment of Mrs. Hurry, which, by-the-by, recalls to my remembrance a story of the German theologian Neander, who, when asked to say grace at a festival, and roast pig was the principal dish, very fervently said, "If Thou can'st bless under the new dispensation what Thou did'st curse under the old, graciously bless this leedle pig." Beyond the piggery is the Haugh Brewery, which time prevents us from inspecting. At the gate loading his cart with draff is little Angus Macdonald, farmer, from Lilyfield. He is a hard-working and industrous man, and is well known in the district. He is saying to his "laad" Archie, "Haste you home with this load, as I want you to go into the town the nicht yet," while the lad, who evidently means to live to be a supple old man, says, "'Deed no, I want to keep some strength for my old age." On the opposite side from the brewery is "Clay Cottage," the residence of Mr. Fraser, leather merchant, Church Street, "The White Laad." We are near the neat grocery establishment of Mr. Alexander Fraser, who takes a prominent part in temperance work in town. Between the roadway and the riverside is the cottage and byre of old Widow Fraser, who is at this moment, as you can see, "putting in" her cow for the night. That shop on the right is occupied by Mr. Macdonald, dyer. The two fine young lads who have passed us on their way home are Angus and John Beaton, sons of Mr. Beaton, farmer, Balnahaun. We have returned to the southern base of the Castle Hill, and will step up View Place, the buildings of which are substantial and commodious. It may interest you to know that on this site several prominent buildings are shown in Sleazer's engraving of Inverness, published in 1693, but those we now see are of a quite modern design. As we at length have made the circuit of the town, we might well afford to bring our walk to an end here, but we will have one more stroll together, embracing part of the Hill district, also the Castle and the Castle Hill, finishing up at the Exchange.

NOTE.—The Ness Islands, so beautifully situated nearly a mile west from the town, have been for a long time a favourite resort of the townspeople in quest of fresh air and recreation. It is recorded that in the olden time, when the Lords of Justiciary came to town and got through with their work of trying offenders, the Provost, Bailies, and other officials of the town used to invite their Lordships to a banquet, which was laid out in some shady nook or grassy slope. The viands consisted principally of trout and salmon caught on the spot, and washed down with an abundant supply of Hollands gin. The purveyors, it is said, were not too particular in squaring with the revenue officer or even with the petty customs. It is particularly gratifying that within recent years the Town-Council has been so careful in seeing that every opportunity is taken to improve and sustain the amenities of this beautiful and healthy resort, which is in all seasons such a source of pleasure, not only to townspeople, but to visitors, who ever delight to wander by its grassy slopes and sylvan bowers, and watch the crystal stream pass over its pebbly bed onward to the sea. Near the west end of the upper bridge is situate the beautiful spring of water popularly known as the " General's Well," presumably named after General Wade, whose name is so much associated with road-making in the Highlands during the last century. The substantial stone work was placed over the well some years ago by the late Provost Grant of Bught.

CHAPTER XXXIII.

NORTH END OF CULDUTHEL ROAD—CASTLE HILL—
CASTLE WYND—EXCHANGE.

As this is the day upon which we are to bring our wanderings to a close, we have, I think, done well in meeting one another in the forenoon rather than the afternoon, because, although there is not much ground to cover, there are many things of interest to note. We are now exactly at the spot (the top of Castle Street, where we first met, and before visiting the Castle Hill, will walk up the brae to the end of Culduthel Road. Here comes Old Mackay, the carter, with his slouched hat pulled well down over his eyes as usual, and wearing his well-worn canvas " smock " or " overalls," which at once indicate the hardy son of toil. He is, as you observe, in charge of his " camel," and is on his way to Strathnairn for a load of stones. Both man and horse are, as you can see, labouring under the weight of many years. We are now at the top of the brae. That low building with the dome, on the slight eminence at the corner of Edinburgh Road, was built for an observatory, the foundation-stone being laid with masonic honours at the same time as that of the Castle, but as astronomy and meteorology are sciences which do not interest the majority of the people, the idea of star-gazing and weather prognosticating have been abandoned. Indeed the majority of folk have enough to do with things on *terra firma* without roaming, even in imagination, through space.

The house has now been turned into a girls' school, which is very much more to the purpose, I think. It is conducted by Miss Anderson. There is little Ann Ellen Hardie from Castle Street, tripping lightly up the steps, while in her hand she carries a practically finished " sampler," of which she is evidently very proud. Directly opposite the Observatory on the other corner of the road is Viewhill, the handsome residence and office of Mr. Joseph Mitchell, C.E., Surveyor of the Highland Roads and Bridges. That stout well-built gentleman who has just passed in is Mr. George Grant Mackay, his principal assistant. Let us walk up the steps into the grounds, and have a look at the front of the building for a moment. Yonder smart young gentleman dressed in velveteens, who is amusing himself on the lawn, is Mr. Mitchell's only son, Master James. Observe over the main entrance is the well-known quotation from " Macbeth "—

> " This Castle hath a pleasant seat : the air
> - Nimbly and sweetly commends itself
> Unto our gentle senses." ·

and over the side entrance gateway the motto " Sapiens qui assiduus."

We will, I think, now retrace our steps. It would entail too much walking to travel over the entire hill, which is sparsely populated, there being but an odd villa here and an isolated cottage there throughout the locality, although it will doubtless in years to come be one of the most popular residential districts about the town, and rightly so, for the situation is admirable. Here comes another well-known carter, William Macdonald, leading his steed by the head up the brae. Though well up in years, he is still active and industrious. A native of Ferintosh, he was in his early days an expert in illicit distillation, and could, if he chose, tell of many stirring escapes from the gaugers. Indeed, if I mistake not, he did get into their clutches once. The other man who is walking alongside him is James Sim, a fine old clarionet player in the militia band. We are back at the entrance to the Castle Hill. The spur of the hill to the left has only recently been annexed by the county authorities. A few paces from the gate here is the scene of the Battle of the Kebbock, which took place on 18th August 1665, and which I will try to describe to you in the language of an historian of the time, the Rev. James Fraser of Brea :—

"One, Finlay Dhu, a townsman, taking up a cheese in his hand, asked what the rate of it was. This being told him, whether designedly or by negligence, he let the cheese drop out of his hand, and down the hill it runs into the river. The woman told him she would oblige him to pay ; he (a crabbed fellow) gaved her cross language of defiance. One that stood by, espousing the quarrel, held him fast, and took off his bonnet in pledge until he should pay the woman. A relation of Finlay's challenged this man, as it was none of his concern. 'Yes,' said he, 'I am concerned as a witness to see just things.' To threatening words they go, and from words to blows, till at length most of the hill market is engaged in a confusion. This alarms the whole town ; the guards are called, who come in arms, and Joe Reed, a pretty man, their captain, runs in betwixt the parties to separate them. Several other gentlemen present offer their mediation, but no hearing. Swords were drawn, guns presented, and some wounds given. Provost Alexander Cuthbert is told that his guards were not regarded ; he puts on a steel cap, sword, and targe, causes ring the alarum bell, and comes straight to the hill, and many pretty fellows with him. The people

P

cry for justice; the guards, being oppressed and abused, let off some shot, and two men are killed outright, and above ten wounded. The noise is hushed and matters examined; the guard is blamed. The Provost in a fury said he allowed and avowed what was done; for who durst disturb the King's free burgh at a market time."

It is said that the dairymaid used to avow that when separating the curds from the whey in making this particular cheese, her hands appeared to be stained to a crimson hue, as if indicative of the strife of which it was the cause. Having now reached the plateau at the west front of the Castle, let us pause for a moment and view the glorious scene that stretches out in panoramic grandeur before us. Below are the silvery waters of the Ness as they ripple o'er their stony bed towards the sea. Away to the right rise hoary Peter's Rock, Craig Phadric, of druidical fame, height 1156 feet; Craig Dunain, hill of the singing birds, height 974 feet, on whose lofty summit may be seen a stately array of tall rock pines like tossing plumes. Then there are the lesser heights of Tomnahurich and Torvean, while to westward lies the great glen of Caledonia, and in the distance, amid a sea of mist, tower the gloomy, sentinel-like peaks on both sides of what may be aptly called the most romantic of Scottish lochs, Loch Ness, yonder conical shaped mountain on the Glen Urquhart side being the far-famed Mealfourvonie. Language completely fails me in attempting to describe to you this glorious scene, but it needs no description, for there before us it is in all its beauty. Of the Ness and the Valley of the Ness it may well be said—

"O! lovely Ness, had Scotia's bard
Woo'd and won and loved beside thee,
Wandered o'er thy grassy sward
Or verdant slopes in youthful glee.

Enshrined in poetry's page to-day,
O'er all the earth thy praise w'd ring,
The 'Clach' abroad in accents gay
Thy beauties unsurpassed would sing."

We had better make the circuit of the Castle and
take in the scenery all around. Yonder farm-steading
on the spur of Craig Phàdric is Scorguie (the windy
corner), which marks the termination of the chain of
hills that extend along the north side of the Great Glen.
Beyond that point, again, you see the shimmering
waters of the Beauly Firth, dotted with the brown sails
of the Clachnaharry fishing boats. Right across the
firth is the quaint village of Charleston, to the rear of
which extends " the Mulbuie," a well-known district of
the Black Isle. In the back-ground stands Ben Wyvis,
one of Scotia's loftiest mountains. There it looms in
the distance like some piebald monster, the zephyrs of
spring having only but partially denuded it of its
wintry mantle.

We are pretty well round the Castle now, but at
every step a fresh view breaks on our gaze. That well-
wooded eminence on the opposite side of the ferry is
Ord Hill, rich in legendary lore, while the little
scattered hamlet which dots its western flank is Craig-
ton, the home of those hardy toilers of the deep, the
Kessock pilots. Situated on the beach a little bit
farther up is the village of North Kessock. The
outlook is now an eastern one, and the broad waters of
the firth, in all their fullness from shore to shore, is
spread before us as they stretch down towards Chanonry
and Fort-George, and then widen out beyond into the
Moray Firth. There is the smoke of one of the trading
steamers as she passes the Fort on her way into port,
while down opposite Avoch is an outward-bound
schooner under full canvas. On the right, a few

miles distant, is the rising ground upon which stands
Drumossie Moor, while beyond are the hills of Nairnshire, and further apace the eastern extremity of the
Grampians.   In turning our eyes from the stretch of
country which surrounds the Castle Hill we may
well say—

> "With these no other scenes compare,
> Mountain, hill, and sea and river,
> No scenes on earth are half so fair,
> On memory's page they're stamped for ever."

We have reached the entrance to the Castle, and
judging from the number of people making their way
into the court-house, I am inclined to think there is
an important trial on.   Oh, here is Mr. Macdonald, the
keeper of the Castle; he will tell us.   "What's the
trial to-day, Mr. Macdonald."   "A poor old fellow from
Stratherrick for sheep stealing.   He is to plead not
guilty, and the trial is to be a jury one.   You should
step in and hear it.   (Walk into court and take seats,
and converse in an undertone.)   The jury which is
now empanelled is composed entirely of well-known
Inverness men, and that is Sheriff Colquhoun on the
bench.   (The trial proceeds, the evidence is concluded,
and the jury retires, while the prisoner, a poor emaci-
ated old man, hangs his head disconsolately in the
dock.)   Here comes the jury now; they haven't taken
long to consider their verdict, considering the fact
that the evidence was of such a contradictory nature.
The foreman has risen to his feet.   Listen!   "We
unanimously find the charge not proven, my Lord."
See how the prisoner brightens up, while a shade of
disappointment overcasts the face of the Fiscal, who to
all appearance had made good the case for the Crown.
We will now get out and go down to the Exchange.
There's William Fraser ("Old Craggie") going down the

Castle Wynd. He was one of the jury, and we will
have a short talk with him about the case. "You
weren't long in giving your verdict in yon case, Mr.
Fraser." "Oh, indeed no! The foreman, Mr. ———,
said as soon as we got into the room, 'It would be far
better to allow the poor old fellow off to get a good
dinner, for he looked as if he needed one, than to send
him to prison for stealing a bit sheepie.' We all agreed;
indeed, we were hungry ourselves." "Well, Mr. Fraser,
the verdict may have been strictly legal and it may
not, but it was certainly a humane one." By the way,
here on the right is one of the most interesting land-
marks in the town, for it is the remains of the outer
wall of the old Castle, while a little farther down on
the same side is one of the most ancient dwelling-houses
in town, as is indicated by the spiral staircase, the small
slated turret, and the pointed windows, the latter with
the usual old-time initials and emblems. Just on the
corner of the Exchange is Mrs. Napier's Commercial
Hotel, from the balcony of which many a stirring
political oration has been delivered. A few yards
distant is the palladium of the burgh, where, like loyal
Clach boys, we will take our last stand. Before parting, however, I may say that although this stone is
known as the "Stone of the Tubs," it is, I believe, of
very much greater antiquity than is generally supposed,
and might properly be rendered "Clach na Culdees,"
which means "The Stone of the Worshippers of God."
Even in our own day this seems an appropriate name
for it, as time and again the Gospel is being proclaimed
from it by those who feel that they have the message
to their fellows. As we bid each other adieu on this
venerable spot, let us unite in wishing that this ancient
and royal burgh may long flourish BY THE PREACHING
OF THE WORD.

NOTE.—Mealfourvonie, height 2700 feet (the hill of the cold blast), is situated about five miles west from Drumnadrochit, and opposite the pier at Foyers, across Loch Ness. The summit may be gained by easy ascent from Glen Urquhart. It is rather interesting to note that this eminence is the first land-mark that the mariner descries when he enters the Moray Firth.

The view from the Castle Hill on a clear day is very striking. A great deal has been written about the Castle at Inverness, and it is said much of its history has been lost in the mists of antiquity. The orignal castle, which dated from Pictish times, is supposed to have stood on the ridge towards the east of the town still called "the Crown." Here, it is said, St. Columba visited Brude, the king of the Northern Picts, about the year 565, and by a startling miracle converted the king to Christianity. Here also, if Hector Boece may be credited, Macbeth, the ambitious Marmoar of Moray, murdered the gracious Duncan. Holinshed in his "Chronicles," published in 1577, repeated Boece's story, and Shakespeare made Holinshed's tale the foundation for the tragedy of Macbeth. It is supposed that Malcolm Canmore, to avenge his father's murder, destroyed the ancient castle, and built in its place the fortress on Castle Hill, which was for many centuries an important post held occasionally by the English soldiers in early times, and often visited by the kings of Scotland.

During the Civil War in 1649, the Royalists took the Castle, dismantled it, and left the place in ruins. Knowing the importance of the place, Cromwell directed the citadel of Inverness to be built, 1652-55; but in 1661 the Scottish Parliament ordered that all the forts built by the English should be razed, and this was among the number. The remains of the olden castle were repaired by the Jacobites at the Revolution, 1688, and held by them for a short time, but it subsequently fell into the hands of the Hanoverians, and was occupied as a fortress by the Government in 1718. After being put into a thorough state of repair, it was called Fort-George. In the rising of 1745 the fortress was occupied by a garrison commanded by Sir John Cope. When Prince Charlie with his Highlanders arrived at Inverness after his retreat from England in February 1746, he captured the Castle and destroyed it, to prevent it falling into the hands of the Royalists. The work of destruction was so complete, that the ruined fortress became a blot on the landscape. After some time the vaulted chambers on the ground floor were duly taken possession of. Two careful tradesmen, the one a weaver and the other a wright, who were in search of work-places at a cheap rate, found their way to occupy the dreary chambers in the Castle. Like every other historic ruin we hear of, the Inverness Castle had a ghost. Although some baronial piles could, and can even still, boast of high-born visitors from the spirit world, such as "dukes and earls an' a' that," the old Castle could only trot out a modest major, who may have come to grief in the mediæval times, if we are to judge from the dress which he is said to have assumed. He was not so obtrusive as some ghosts we hear of, if we are to believe the tale that is told regarding his appearances. It seems that one particular night the wright was working overtime when "the Major" stepped into the apartment in order to see how he was getting on. Next morning, in relating the adventure of the previous evening, "Chips" was asked what he did when he beheld the visitor. "Well," said he coolly, "I simply minded my own business." Afterwards "mind your own business like the wright when the ghost visited

him" became a trite saying in town. The Castle
remained in a ruinous condition until it ultimately fell
in 1790, as referred to by John M'Lean, the nonagenarian, in his story. The stones of the old building
were speedily removed, and for well-nigh half a century
the summit of the Hill was as bare as a bowling-green.
A flagstaff being erected on it, and on the King's
birthday a flag might have been seen gaily floating
from it. The county commissioners erected the present
Castle from designs by Cousins, of Edinburgh, at a cost
of £15,000, the style being purely baronial, and contains
a spacious court-room, a grand entrance and staircase
leading to the offices above. There are few court-rooms
in the country to compare withit. In the landing on
the staircase is a fine marble bust of Sheriff Patrick
Fraser Tytler, while in the main apartment is a full-
length portrait of the Right Honourable Charles Grant,
by Raeburn.

Mr. Grant was a very prominent politician in the
early part of the century, and represented the county
in Parliament for many years. His father was born at
Aldourie farmhouse on the day of the Battle of Culloden ;
his grandfather, being engaged in the battle, was
numbered among the slain. His father having received
an appointment in the East India Company's service,
repaired thither with his family, and in course of time
attained to a high position in the government of that
country. His son Charles, if I mistake not, subsequently became secretary of the administration, while
his eldest son, Sir Robert, attained to the position of
Governor of Bombay. Returning home, Charles was
elected Member of Parliament for the county in
succession to his father. In April 1829 he voted in
favour of "The Catholic Emancipation Bill." On receipt
of the news of the passing of the bill in Inverness an anti-

Catholic demonstration was got up, when the populace took occasion to burn the county member in effigy. Three years thereafter Mr. Grant voted in favour of the " Reform Bill " (1832), and on his next visit to Inverness he was received with great acclamation. A chair of state being provided, the now popular member was carried on the shoulders of the townsmen in procession through the streets. Having served the county and his party with much acceptance, he was subsequently raised to the peerage as Lord Glenelg, and lived well into the century. In addition to being an able administrator, his brother, Sir Robert, was a hymn-writer of considerable merit, and is the author of the well-known favourite hymn commencing—

> " O worship the King, all glorious above,
> O gratefully sing His power and His love."

At the time the Castle was built, 1835, the Hill was much neglected, but within recent years there has been a great improvement. In 1856 Mr. Kennedy Macnab asked the Government for a couple of Sebastapol big guns, a number of which had been brought home as trophies of war, so that they might be placed on the Hill. Mr. Macnab's application was granted, but the Town-Council declined to have anything to do with the matter, and the result was that Mr. Henry J. Baillie, Member of Parliament for the county, was approached by Mr. Macnab, and very generously defrayed the expense of the carriage. The council ultimately becoming alive to the matter, gave orders to have the guns removed from the Thornbush to their present position on the Castle Hill, where they arrived by steamer with all the pomp and circumstance the occasion demanded. Bailie Cook's shipbuilders gave valuable assistance in connection with the removal.

Before bidding adieu to the Castle, the hope may be
expressed that in the not very distant future the
authorities may see their way to make an entrance to
the Castle Hill from Ness Bank at the north corner of
the Hill, near the building now known as Castle Tolmie.
This is a much-needed want, and would, in addition to
improving the amenities of the locality, prove a great
boon to visitors and residenters.   At the time referred
to in " the walk " there were only a few cottages in the
Barnhill district, while Mr. Thomas Fraser was lessee
of Abertarff Farm, which is now known as the Crown
district, and is densely populated.   The only building
of interest on the Hill was the Raining School, which
derived its name from Dr. Raining, a Norwich merchant
and philanthropist.   It was erected in 1747 by the
" Society for Promoting Christian Knowledge."   Among
other things taught was the art of spinning.   It has
rendered good service in its day, and although it is not
now a beacon of learning, it has still its uses.   Much
has been written regarding the Clachnacuddin Stone,
and it almost seems unnecessary to say very much
upon the subject.   As is well known, it was used by
the maidens and housewives as a resting place for their
" stoups " when on their way from the river with their
daily supply of water.   There they were wont to be met
by the young men, who usually hung in groups around
the spot, and it may with safety be inferred that many
a choice bit of local gossip was retailed at these
meetings.   It may be mentioned that for many years
the shaft of the Town Cross lay in what is known as the
Session Park, near the present site of the High School.
In the thirties it was taken and placed in front of the
old Town Hall, a little to the west of its present
position, while the Clachnacuddin Stone, which lay on
the edge of the pavement, was placed beneath it.   Both

have been shifted, even separated more than once, but again they are united, thanks to our distinguished burgh member, Sir R. B. Finlay, K.C., P.C., Attorney-General of England, and in their present position they will doubtless remain for centuries to come, and until the surrounding buildings are razed through the ravages of time.

Dear old Clach! hoary with the lapse of ages, a witness of bygone days in the Highland capital, the scene of many a strange old-time gathering, and destined yet to behold the distant future. Is it any wonder that Invernessians in every land revere it, and when speaking of their native town point to "the Clach" as the loadstone of their affections?

CHAPTER XXXIV.

THE GREAT FLOOD, JANUARY 25TH, 1849.

As the generation that lived in the middle of the last century, and who remember what has long locally been known as the "great flood," is fast passing away, a brief narrative of that calamity may aptly close my reminiscences. I may here remark that subsequent to that event the physical features of the town have been very much changed. The banks of the river have been considerably raised, widened, and strengthened. All the then existing bridges have been removed, and those that have taken their place are of a much more substantial nature, so that, in the event of another such occurrence, the exposure to the waters and the damage would be much less severe. The winter of 1848-9 was observed to be unusually stormy,—a good deal of wind and rain with snow,—indeed, what might be considered very unsettled weather. It was a source of great thankfulness to God that the area of the flood was not extensive or far-reaching, and although there was much danger, yet no lives were lost. The leading feature of the calamity was the destruction of the old stone bridge, which formed the connecting link between the east and west sides of the river and the north and south of Scotland, and which for 165 years had nobly breasted the winter storms. It was swept away in the midst of circumstances which were calculated to awaken the most intense interest in the safety of the many persons exposed to danger. I remember crossing

the bridge two days before its yielding to the great
stress of water borne down against its piers, and
observed the ominous looks that were exchanged when
discussing the ever-recurring topic of the safety of the
structure, fears being freely expressed that it could not
bear up against the rising flood. Referring to the
subject of the cause of the flood, the late Mr. Joseph
Mitchell informs us "that heavy rains continued to fall
over the upper country for three consecutive days, with
violent squalls of wind, and the Ness rose to an unpre-
cedented height, overflowing its banks and submerging
about a third of the town, particularly on the west
side, where the flood rose to the depth of from two to
over three feet." Meantime the attention of the Canal
authorities was directed to the unsafe state of the
locks at Dochgarroch, which appeared to be in danger
of being swept away by the intense pressure of the
stream, thus exposing the west part of the town to an
inundation from both sides, and increasing the already
too strained feeling of alarm among the people in this
particular locality. Mr. George May, Canal superin-
tendent, with a large staff of workmen, concentrated
their efforts at this point, and by setting up a substantial barricade and using every means to strengthen
the locks, and by keeping constant watch until the
waters began to recede, the danger at this point was
happily averted. Continuing the narrative, another
writer says, "The Ness began to rise with alarming
rapidity on Wednesday, the 24th, and by nightfall
the volume created a feeling of intense uneasiness
among the part of the community most liable to
be affected by an overflow. It was destined to be a
night to be long remembered. As midnight approached
the waters were still rising. Few lights went out in
those streets which were within reach of the noisy

torrent. People began to patrol the river banks, anxiously noticing the increase of the waters. Crowds gathered on and near the bridge, which trembled under their feet, as the flood swept through the arches with angry roar at the obstruction the piers formed to its majestic progress. The whole outlook was threatening; squalls of wind from the west and the north-west were frequent, and the rain fell incessantly. As the tide was at its height at one o'clock, it was hoped that the river would decrease as the waters of the tide retired. The slender hope was, however, soon to be abandoned, as the river kept on increasing while the tide fell; it became evident that the flood, high as it was, had not yet obtained its maximum. The night watchmen were called in from their beats. The day force were aroused, and special constables were engaged to assist in the work of removal, which began to become general, as well as to protect as far as possible the property more immediately exposed, rousing those who had gone to rest, and assisting others to remove furniture from the lower to the upper apartments of their houses. From three o'clock till five on the morning of Thursday, the 25th, the river still increased. At the latter hour it had surrounded the houses in the upper part of Ness Bank to the depth of nearly two feet, and penetrating the drains, it flooded the lower rooms. In a few minutes more it had risen over the doorsteps, and overflowed in a rapidly increasing stream through the houses. Now the water reached the Haugh Road, down which it ran in a rapid stream from the head of the Ladies' Walk, covering the gardens and fields adjacent. A small house standing between the road and the river was the first to be abandoned. The water having nearly reached the thatch, the inmates were removed to the shelter of the higher standing dwellings in the vicinity. At the lower end of Ness Walk a poor widow lost her cow, which was her chief support, so sudden did the waters rush on this exposed part of the town. It now became evident that the bridge could not much longer resist the current. It trembled sensibly, and the water, as it rushed in foam through its groaning arches, is described as awful. At a few minutes before six o'clock, when the flood had almost reached the keystone of the lower arches, the spray was breaking in sheets over the parapet walls. The constable whose duty it was to warn passengers of the danger of crossing observed the exposed half of the small southern arch adjoining Bridge Street give way. In a few seconds it crumbled down and was engulfed. The bridge lamps, which continued to burn till then, went out. A slight moaning sound was heard above the noise of the torrent. The centre arch gave way, and in a minute afterwards all the other arches disappeared beneath the flood, leaving only a portion of the arch next Young Street, with the lamp attached. The obstruction caused by the falling materials for a moment forced back the mighty flow, it rose high over the banks and swept up to the houses in Gordon Place, and then as rapidly receded, and the current rushed on, foaming and boiling in a frightful mass over the fallen fragments of the bridge. Thus fell the good old fabric that so long had breasted the Ness and defied its floods. The last person to cross was Matthew Campbell, a jolly son of Neptune, who was said to be at the time " three sheets in the wind." He was an old academy boy, and won the gold medal for classics in 1833. Coming down Bridge Street immediately before the small arch gave way, and despite the entreaties and physical opposition of the constable, he sprang forward, saying " he would tell the people on

the other side." He lost no time in crossing, but had
just reached the northern bank when the bridge disappeared. Only a few minutes previous the grand-
children of Dr. Rose (who lived in the house now
occupied as the Glenalbyn Hotel) had been seen
crossing in charge of a servant, the doctor himself
intending to follow to seek shelter in some less exposed
situation. The loss of the bridge, however, separated
him and his children without being able to ascertain
whether they had made good their escape. By half-
past six the whole of the Little Green, Tanner's Lane,
King Street, and Huntly Street, northward to the
Green of Muirtown and Merkinch, was flooded to the
depth of from two to three feet. Whenever the inmates
could escape unassisted, they were seen hurrying out,
carrying with them the most valuable of their little
household stores. Mothers and daughters, screaming
with dread, were to be seen half-dressed, and affrighted
children in their arms, leaving their houses and wading
through the still rising waters. Fathers and brothers
assisted in the hasty flight, many of them carrying with
them poor bedridden friends and neighbours, who
had not left their rooms for many a day, until thus
threatened with instant death in their beds. It is
gratifying to observe that all the houses on the higher
grounds, and beyond the immediate reach of the flood,
threw open their doors for the reception of the house-
less, and in the darkness of that fearful morning many
a deed of Christian kindness was done which has never
been recorded. As daylight came on the morning of
the 25th, all the available boats were procured, and
many of the leading townsmen exerted themselves to
the utmost in the work of rescuing the many sufferers.
Two elderly ladies residing in Ness Bank, on being
offered assistance to leave their dwelling, refused to

leave, their modesty not permitting them to be carried out on men's shoulders. After some delay a tub was got, and the distance from the front door to outside the railing was to be made in it, but when halfway the tub capsized, the occupant had to yield her scruples, and both ladies were soon got into the boat. A poor lame fellow, who lived alone in Tomnahurich Street, made signs from an upper window of his desire to be rescued, and was carried into one of the boats, when lo! he found that in the joy of his deliverance he was as helpless as ever, having left behind him his indispensable crutches. As one of the boats was being rowed past the house of "Jamie, the weaver," on the Green, he was requested to come on board. "Oh," replied Jamie, "I am all right up here" (he having got to an upper floor), "but as my fuel is near done, would any of you gentlemen be so good as bring me a ha'penny worth of peats?" The only connection between the banks of the river was by the Black Bridge, and grave doubts were entertained with regard to its safety. Constables were stationed to prevent more than two persons crossing at the same time. Meantime the Magistrates set about making temporary provision for the refugees. The large kitchen of the Northern Meeting Rooms was being fitted up to receive the men. Dr. Bell's Institution and the Poorhouse were similarly utilised to accommodate the women and children, while the Guildry Room, which was situated over the old Town Hall, was used as an orderly room, from whence the workers received their instructions, and in which they found occasional food and rest. In the morning I remember being taken down Bridge Street just as a party of workmen had finished putting a strong barricade across the street from Gordon Place to Castle Tolmie, which nearly abutted on to the river. I

Q

could hear the roar and rush of the stream as it flowed
over the ruins of the bridge. In the afternoon I was
taken to the Castle Hill, where a number of people
were assembled. The view from this coign of vantage
was at once awesome and sublime. Looking upwards
the river was seen descending in the height of a
turbulent flood, extending in breadth from the Haugh
Road nearly up to the door of the Northern Infirmary,
and the houses in Ness Bank seemed as if placed in
the middle of a stream, the water in the Haugh Road
being now three feet in depth. A boat was drawn up
at the foot of View Place, the work of rescue having
now been completed. Looking over the river an
immense breach was observed to have been made in
the high wall of the garden of Ness House, through
which the water rushed over the whole garden, while
the ground floor of the house was completely sub-
merged. Looking down the stream the spectacle was
still more strange and striking. Streets flooded, houses
deserted, and here and there an arm extended from an
upper window, waving signals possibly of distress or
for assistance from without, the bridge gone, the roadway seemingly undermined, and the old house at the
foot of Bridge Street hanging over the raging stream as
if to drop into the current which was rolling onward,
sweeping past shop doors and houses as if these formed
its natural banks. In three days the waters began to
recede, and the people gradually began to return to
their disordered houses, which they right earnestly set
about to get put in proper order. Through the generosity of the sympathetic public a plentiful supply of
coal was provided for the poorer people, and anon
things began to look up again. The high retaining
wall below the Castle Hill, which was erected only a
few years before at the suggestion of Provost Nicol,

was found to be of great value in preventing the hill from being undermined. The Town-Council and Road Trustees have subsequently, in their wisdom, steadily sought, as means would permit, to raise the river banks several feet in places which appeared to be more immediately exposed. So that, in the event of another such visitation, the danger to inhabitants and property would be reduced to a minimum. Since the occurrence which I have thus recorded in the foregoing chapter, as the result of both private and public enterprise, great improvements have been effected on the lands on the west side of the river. Many excellent roads and streets have been laid out and built upon, so that the locality may now be considered as one of the finest residential quarters of the town.

EDINBURGH : PRINTED BY JAMES SKINNER AND COMPANY.

Milton Keynes UK
Ingram Content Group UK Ltd.
UKHW050657261123
433027UK00021B/116